Anyone contemplating or engaged in health-related research should read this book. The first step in research is to learn what came before, a step that is ever more challenging as knowledge expands. Hempel distills methods for carrying out comprehensive, unbiased, and valid literature reviews, and applies them to common review tasks. This book is the best I have seen for introducing readers clearly and succinctly to the discipline of systematic evidence review.

—**Lisa V. Rubenstein, MD, MSPH, FACP,** Professor Emeritus of Medicine and Public Health, UCLA, and Senior Scientist, RAND, Los Angeles, CA

This book provides an excellent introduction to different kinds of literature reviews and guides readers through the steps involved in systematic reviews. Practical aspects are illustrated by examples of fictional students working on a literature review. This approach, benefitting from Hempel's wealth of experience, makes this a highly recommended book for anyone considering to prepare a literature review.

—**Jos Kleijnen, MD, PhD,** Professor of Systematic Reviews in Health Care, Maastricht University, The Netherlands

Conducting Your Literature Review

Concise Guides to Conducting Behavioral, Health, and Social Science Research Series

Conducting Your Literature Review
  Susanne Hempel

Designing and Proposing Your Research Project
  Jennifer Brown Urban and Bradley Matheus Van Eeden-Moorefield

Managing Your Research Data and Documentation
  Kathy R. Berenson

Writing Your Psychology Research Paper
  Scott A. Baldwin

Conducting Your Literature Review

SUSANNE HEMPEL

CONCISE GUIDES TO CONDUCTING BEHAVIORAL, HEALTH, AND SOCIAL SCIENCE RESEARCH

AMERICAN PSYCHOLOGICAL ASSOCIATION
Washington, DC

Published by
American Psychological Association
750 First Street, NE
Washington, DC 20002
https://www.apa.org

Order Department
https://www.apa.org/pubs/books
order@apa.org

In the U.K., Europe, Africa, and the Middle East, copies may be ordered from Eurospan
https://www.eurospanbookstore.com/apa
info@eurospangroup.com   .

Typeset in Minion by Circle Graphics, Inc., Reisterstown, MD

Printer: Sheridan Books, Chelsea, MI
Cover Designer: Naylor Design, Washington, DC

Library of Congress Cataloging-in-Publication Data

Names: Hempel, Susanne, author.
Title: Conducting your literature review / by Susanne Hempel.
Description: Washington, DC : American Psychological Association, [2020] |
    Series: Concise guides to conducting behavioral, health, and social
    science research series | Includes bibliographical references and index.
Identifiers: LCCN 2019011722 (print) | LCCN 2019980880 (ebook) | ISBN
    9781433830921 (paperback) | ISBN 1433830922 (paperback) | ISBN
    9781433831232 (ebook) | ISBN 1433831236 (ebook)
Subjects: LCSH: Psychology—Research—Methodology. |
    Psychology—Information resources. | Psychology—Authorship. | Social
    sciences—Research—Methodology.
Classification: LCC BF76.5 .H45 2010 (print) | LCC BF76.5 (ebook) | DDC
    150.72—dc23
LC record available at https://lccn.loc.gov/2019011722
LC ebook record available at https://lccn.loc.gov/2019980880

Printed in the United States of America

http://dx.doi.org/10.1037/0000155-000

10 9 8 7 6 5 4 3 2 1

Contents

CONTENTS

Series Foreword

W hy are you reading this book? Perhaps you have been assigned to write a research paper in an undergraduate course. Maybe you are considering graduate school in one of the behavioral, health, or social science disciplines, such as psychology, public health, nursing, or medicine, and know that having a strong research background gives you a major advantage in getting accepted. Maybe you simply want to know how to conduct research in these areas. Or perhaps you are interested in actually conducting your own study. Regardless of the reason, you are probably wondering, "How do I start?"

Conducting research can be analogous to cooking a meal for several people. Doing so involves planning (e.g., developing a menu), having adequate resources (e.g., having the correct pots, pans, carving knives, plates), knowing what the correct ingredients are (e.g., what spices are needed), properly cooking the meal (e.g., grilling vs. baking, knowing how long it takes to cook), adequately presenting the food (e.g., making the meal look appetizing), and so forth. Conducting research also involves planning, proper execution, having adequate resources, and presenting one's project in a meaningful manner. Both activities also involve creativity, persistence, caring, and ethical behavior. But just as with cooking a meal for several people, conducting research should follow one of my favorite pieces of advice: "Remember that the devil is in the details." If you want your dinner guests to find your meal tasty, you need to follow a recipe properly and measure the ingredients accurately (e.g., too much or too little of various ingredients can make the entrée taste awful). Similarly, conducting research without properly paying attention to details can lead to erroneous results.

Okay, but what about your question, "How do I start?" This American Psychological Association book series provides detailed but user-friendly guides for conducting research in the behavioral, health, and social sciences from start to finish. I cannot help but think of another food analogy here—that is, the series will focus on everything from "soup to nuts." These short, practical books guide you, the student/researcher, through each stage of the process of developing, conducting, writing, and presenting a research project. Each book focuses on a single aspect of research, such as choosing a research topic, following ethical guidelines when conducting research with humans, using appropriate statistical tools to analyze data, and deciding which measures to use in your project. Each volume in this series will help you attend to the details of a specific activity. All volumes will help you complete important tasks and include illustrative examples. Although the theory and conceptualization behind each activity is important to know, these books especially focus on the "how to" of conducting research, so that you, the research student, can successfully carry out a meaningful research project.

This volume, by Susanne Hempel, focuses on conducting literature reviews. As she notes, a *literature review* is an overview of the available research in a given area. Undertaking such a review can be a challenging endeavor. For example, there are several different reasons for conducting a literature review. If you have read journal articles describing a particular investigation, you know that a literature review can provide background for the research study included in the paper's introduction. A review can also stand alone, summarizing a group of research studies focused on a given topic. Hempel does an excellent job of helping the reader to engage in each step of the literature review process from start to finish.

So, the answer to the question "How do I start?" is simple: Just turn the page and begin reading!

Best of luck!

—Arthur M. Nezu, PhD, DHL, ABPP
Series Editor

Acknowledgments

I would like to thank my students, who helped me identify the material used in this book; funding agencies that have commissioned and inspired pragmatic solutions for literature reviews; and my family— Jeremy, Alexander, and Daniel Miles—for their support. I also thank William Shadish and Arthur Nezu for their support and helpful suggestions.

Conducting
Your Literature
Review

Introduction

A *literature review* is an overview of the available research for a specific scientific topic. Literature reviews summarize existing research to answer a review question, provide the context for new research, or identify important gaps in the existing body of literature. We now have access to lots of research and know a lot about literature reviews as a scientific method. For students in psychology and the social sciences, conducting a literature review provides a fantastic opportunity to use the existing research evidence and to do so in a way that parallels the methods used to design and execute primary research. However, to do that effectively, it is important to learn strategies for conducting a literature review that leads to reliable and valid conclusions about the research literature.

http://dx.doi.org/10.1037/0000155-001
Conducting Your Literature Review, by S. Hempel

TYPES OF LITERATURE REVIEWS

Literature reviews come in different types and formats. All literature reviews are secondary literature because they summarize existing research evidence, that is, primary research. But reviews can serve different functions and use literature very differently.

First, a review may be part of a larger piece of work, such as the background section of a research article, or it may be a stand-alone product with its own research merit, such as a review article. And then there are many different types of stand-alone literature reviews. Traditional literature reviews, or *narrative reviews*, usually aim to give either an overview or an introduction to a research field. An *expert review* relies heavily on the expertise of the author. Scientific journals may approach a key expert in a research field to write a review ("by invitation only") and ask this expert for their take on the research topic. *Critical reviews* do not necessarily try to provide a general overview or neutral summary of the existing research; instead, they primarily cite research results to convey a specific message. *Systematic reviews* follow a standardized research methodology that systematically collates and synthesizes existing evidence. Systematic reviews aim to answer a research or policy question with existing research, using rigorous reporting and applying many steps to reduce reviewer errors and bias. *Meta-analyses* summarize published studies statistically by aggregating data across studies. They are often based on a systematic review of the literature. Likewise, many systematic reviews summarize the results of included studies through meta-analysis, also called *statistical pooling*.

This book focuses on the steps needed to conduct a systematic literature review and includes tips for modifying or leaving out steps as needed depending on your audience, purpose, and goal.

WHAT YOU WILL LEARN FROM THIS BOOK

Literature reviews have changed a lot over time and are now much more demanding than just 10 years ago because of the sheer volume of published research. We have access to more research than ever before, and the rate of scientific publication as well as database indexing has accelerated considerably in recent years. As just one example, I searched the database PubMed (a process you'll learn more about in Chapter 2) for the term *personality* and found that in early 2019 more than 400,000 articles were published on that topic, whereas in 2003 only half of that number existed (see Figure 1). When you embark on a literature review, you will almost always find a huge amount of available research literature. Reviewing all of it is challenging, and a structured approach is required to handle the volume. This book will help you formulate a strategy within which you can make clear decisions about what to include and not include in your review and thus avoid getting washed away by the torrent of available research.

In addition, our knowledge about literature reviews has also increased. For one thing, we know more now about threats to the validity of literature reviews, that is, factors that contribute to a wrong or misleading overview of the literature. Consequently, we have a better understanding of the steps that are needed to

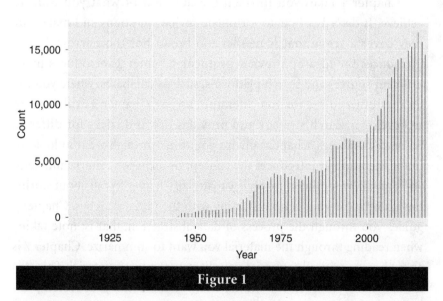

Figure 1

Number of citations published per year reporting on an example research topic (personality).

produce a reliable and unbiased summary of the existing research. This book will walk you through those steps one by one. Each chapter targets a specific part or stage in the literature review. Throughout this book, the elements and reporting structure of a systematic review serve as a framework for literature reviews.

The first four chapters of this book are about identifying material for your literature review, the next four chapters are about what to do with the material that you have assembled, and the final chapter is dedicated to documenting it all. Continuing the cooking metaphor from Arthur M. Nezu's series foreword, think about Chapters 1 through 4 as planning your meal, going shopping, and getting the ingredients. Chapters 5 through 8 are where the actual cooking happens: preparing the food, chopping, and frying. And Chapter 9 is about serving the meal. Each chapter introduces you first to the general ideas or concepts that are important for the step in the literature review. It then explains the procedure and its purpose and outlines the ways to operationalize the step, that is, how you can translate it into conducting your literature review.

Chapter 1 takes you through the question of what you want to achieve. It describes how to formulate review questions and make sure they cover a scope that is neither too broad nor too narrow. It also introduces the idea of a review protocol. Chapter 2 introduces many different sources and search platforms, such as databases, where you can locate studies to use for your literature review. Chapter 3 explains how to develop a search strategy and provides tips and tricks for different research databases. Chapter 4 helps you think through what to look for in the literature. It introduces the concept of inclusion criteria and helps you organize your literature review material. Chapter 5 is all about storing the material for your review, starting with the initial searches. Chapter 6 guides you through the process of data abstraction, that is, note taking when reading through the material you want to summarize. Chapter 7 is about how to critically appraise your literature review material. This step is important because not all the material you include in your review plays an equal role in answering your review question. Some material is the cake, as it were, and other material is the frosting or decoration. Chapter 8 is all about your synthesis, your summary of the literature and your answers to the review questions. Chapter 9 is dedicated to translating everything you have done so far into your actual write-up and how to best document your review process and present the results of your literature review.

At times I might point you to a future chapter or a chapter already covered. This is because a literature review is not a fully linear process. Think of it as an iterative process. For example, while reading Chapter 4 on what literature to include, you might reflect on your own in-progress project and realize there was another entire database you intended to search, which would then take you back to Chapter 2, the chapter on where to look for information.

You will see that there are several ways to approach a literature review, as well as different types of literature reviews, and the level of effort and analysis, as well as what sections to include in your final write-up, depends very much on your goal, purpose, and audience for your review. To help you with the decisions, each chapter includes an example of a fictional student who is working on a literature review and who takes a particular approach that fits the purpose of their assignment. Watch out for a text box and the student icon:

Each chapter ends with a series of action steps that you can use as a checklist for your progress. Each chapter provides a lot of information—in some cases maybe more than you had hoped—and the checklist is meant as a tool for deciding the crucial steps. You can also use the checklist items as a guide for ongoing communication with others who may be involved in your project, such as professors, research partners, reference librarians, or subject matter experts, or documenting your progress. Just keep in mind that you may sometimes need to read ahead and then come back to an action step to complete it. This is because of the iterative nature of literature reviews.

There really is no one-method-fits-all approach to literature reviews. Instead, throughout the book, I try to equip you with methods and tools so that you can select the best ones for your specific literature review project. Every chapter describes an important step for conducting literature reviews, but all chapters address different types of reviews and levels of effort. The action steps at the end will help you identify the essential steps that apply to all literature reviews.

GUIDING THEMES

Throughout the book are two overall guiding themes. In terms of the big picture, as well as for many specific decisions, one critical theme is to match the conduct and documentation of the literature review to its purpose as well as to the review question you want to answer. The other critical theme is that the literature review process should be transparent and carefully thought through, just like any other scientific work.

You will see throughout the book that I emphasize the scientific nature of a literature review and that I am guiding you through a structured process. The steps in this book are designed to help you draw reliable and valid conclusions about the literature. Literature reviews are susceptible to two main sources of *bias* (i.e., processes that can distort the conclusions of the review):

- selection bias
- reporting bias

Selection bias occurs when you are using a bad selection of the existing literature. Your review does not need to find each and every paper ever published on the topic, but it should not be misleading. Literature reviews can be misleading when they leave out whole categories of studies that could shed light on the review question or when they look at only a haphazard selection of studies. Accordingly, Chapters 1 through 4 are about finding the right material for your review.

Reporting bias occurs when you are summarizing the literature in an unbalanced, inconsistent, or distorted way. Chapters 5 through 8 are about methods to appropriately synthesize the information in the material you have located.

Throughout the book, you will notice a lot of emphasis on documentation. This is because the literature search process is like any other scientific process—it should be described clearly and, as far as possible, be reproducible. That is, you should be able to explain what process you went through to find the information that is summarized in your review, and someone else replicating your methods and procedures should find the same material. Then you should be able to describe what you did with the material. Similarly, someone else looking at your material should come to similar conclusions about the literature.

My hope is that by providing you with a description of all the steps involved in a literature review, along with examples and tools, I will help make your literature review project achievable and manageable. It can be challenging to sort through a jungle of research and tame your material into a review with its own internal logic and flow. Rest assured, even those of us who conduct multiple literature reviews per year still learn a lot with every review, and every topic is unique. But it does get easier as you gradually internalize the steps involved and apply them to your project. So, let's get to it!

1

What to Achieve: Clarifying the Goal of Your Literature Review

Before you start your literature review, clarify what you want to achieve. This chapter will help you to think through the overall format of your review. I describe how to generate a review question and determine the scope of the review, as well as how to balance breadth and depth when formulating and scoping your review question. Finally, I suggest some reasons to consider using a review protocol, a tool that is especially helpful for larger review projects.

If you were cooking a meal, this would be the planning stage wherein you determine whether you are hosting an elaborate formal dinner party, a simple pizza night with a few friends, or something in between.

http://dx.doi.org/10.1037/0000155-002
Conducting Your Literature Review, by S. Hempel

REVIEW FORMAT

Before you start your review, clarify the goal of conducting the literature review. Ask yourself who is it for, how it will be published, and how much space you have for the write-up—and find all instructions you need to follow. When you are assigned a review or decide to undertake one, determine whether your literature review will be a stand-alone product, part of a research project write-up, or just a short background section (see Figure 1.1). Obviously, the format will influence how you conduct the literature review and how you document your results.

Putting Together a Background Section

If the review is going to serve as the background section for a research article that presents original research, the literature review helps to introduce the topic and place the new research into the context of existing knowledge. Because readers of introductions typically want to get to the core of the article—the research hypothesis and results—the literature review section needs to be carefully curated. Stick to a tight word limit, and be very selective in your material and very brief in what you say about it. For example, you may want to start with identifying the most-cited articles on the topic (see Chapter 2), come up with a highly selective search strategy (see Chapter 3), carefully think through what kind of literature you want to cite (see Chapter 4), and make sure that you get the material into citation management software so that you can cite it easily (see Chapter 5). Plan what you want to say about the material (see Chapter 6), decide which material deserves the most attention (see Chapter 7),

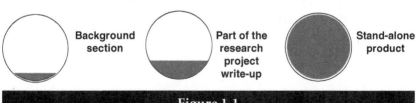

| Background section | Part of the research project write-up | Stand-alone product |

Figure 1.1

Range of literature review types.

and come up with an organizing framework of how to present the literature (see Chapter 8). Chapter 9 offers lots of ideas for what you could present, including definitions, research dilemmas, the state of the research, and how the new research fits into what is already known about the topic.

Producing a Literature Review as Part of Your Thesis

If your literature review is part of a larger research project, you can cover the literature in slightly more breadth and depth than you would for an introduction, but you still need to be selective in how you present the information. As with an introduction, the reader of the overall research report (or your thesis) will want to get to the new research. For example, it might be best to put all methods into an appendix and present only the review findings in the text. Practically, that means that the information about your sources (Chapter 2), your search strategy (Chapter 3), your inclusion criteria (Chapter 4), your literature flow (Chapter 5), your data abstraction strategy (Chapter 6), and how you went about appraising studies (Chapter 7) will not be described in detail in the text. Instead, you will go straight to presenting the results, using the strategies described in Chapter 8 and applying the documentation tips presented in Chapter 9.

Writing a Stand-Alone Literature Review Document

If you are working on a stand-alone literature review project, you will likely have time and resources to make full use of all the procedures described in this book. You will also likely be able to describe everything you did when conducting the review in detail using the standard format of a scientific paper. You can embed your literature review findings in a write-up that has an introduction and method, results, and discussion sections. It will be most helpful to formulate a review question and define the scope as described later in this chapter. You will also benefit the most from writing a review protocol (see the Review Protocol section). You can use multiple sources that are introduced in Chapter 2 and work out an effective search strategy (Chapter 3). Using the strategies in this book, you will be able to think through the literature that is most helpful to answer your review question (Chapter 4), store and organize a high volume of review material (Chapter 5), design a data abstraction scheme (Chapter 6), apply critical appraisal criteria (Chapter 7), and spend time on the analysis of the literature and presentation of the findings of your review (Chapter 8). The last chapter (Chapter 9) gives editorial guidance and ideas for figures and tables for a polished documentation of your literature review.

REVIEW QUESTION

Before you start the review, determine what you want to find out from the literature. A review can have different aims. For example, a literature review may be an overview of the research issues that are relevant to an understanding of the field. Or the review might explore the volume and types of available studies on a topic to describe the state of the research in that area. The purpose of such a review would be to say how large the literature base is or whether the studies on the topic are mainly exploratory or confirmatory. A literature review can also set out to summarize key results of a research field. Some literature reviews specifically aim to identify research gaps.

Systematic reviews start with formulating a review question. This is a good idea for all literature reviews because a review question pinpoints the focus of the review. The review question is something that you are trying to answer using the existing research literature. The question assumes that, at least theoretically, it is possible to give a concrete answer. Here are some examples of review questions: "What are the effects of a specific treatment on a specific outcome measure in a specific population?" and "Do individual differences in toddlers' temperament influence the parenting style of their parents?" Formulating review questions is similar to testing hypotheses—just as you need a hypothesis that can be tested, you need a review question that can be answered.

Formulating a question requires you to be specific about what exactly you want to be able to say based on the research literature. For example, you might decide to carry out a literature review on individual differences.

However, this question is not answerable in a traditional literature review project. The question is too vague and too broad. Researchers have studied many dimensions of individual differences, and endless areas could be affected by individual differences. You need to narrow down the question to something concrete and specific. A better question would be, "Are introverts more successful in terms of salary earnings in coding jobs than are extraverts?" This question acknowledges that many individual differences exist and that it is important to specify the

 Frankie's Family Therapy Review

Frankie listened to Esther Perel's podcast, *Where Should We Begin* (https://www.estherperel.com/podcast), and is now intrigued by systemic therapy. Frankie wants to know more about it but finds a ton of literature on the topic. So, Frankie decides to select one approach (family therapy, a common approach within systemic therapy) and one specific indication (bereavement, a topic very personal to Frankie) and then sets out to formulate a concrete review question ("What are the effects of family therapy on social functioning in the context of bereavement?"). The focused question will ensure that it can be answered, and it is specific enough to keep the review manageable. It specifies (a) the intervention (family therapy), (b) the outcome that will measure the effect (social functioning), and (c) the context or clinical indication (i.e., bereavement) because the question of whether family therapy is helpful may depend on what it is being used for. Frankie knows that social adjustment is a broad field but that *functioning* narrows it down to a specific aspect that can be measured. Frankie acknowledges that results of family therapy will vary a lot depending on what exactly is measured and that *social functioning* needs to be defined (which will be a lot easier after first reading some of the literature).

dimension of interest. The definition of success is critical here so it has been narrowed down to a specific measure. Finally, the setting or context is specified because the answer to the question may vary by the type of vocational category.

A common misstep is to start with a review outline that is too broad. In such a situation, the review is trying to address too much, and it is unlikely that all the evidence can be reviewed within the available time and with the available resources. An easy rule of thumb is that your review question should have three components (see Figure 1.2). Think about the population, the predictor or intervention, and the outcome measures or results you want to address—or any three elements (e.g., context, predictor variable, outcome domain).

Specifying three elements in the review question usually results in a sufficiently specific question that you can work with—otherwise your question is likely to be too broad to be answered clearly, and there will be far too much literature to review.

REVIEW SCOPE

The scope of the review describes what it covers and, just as important, what it does not cover. First, your review scope defines the topic you are reviewing. It is absolutely critical that the reader of your literature review

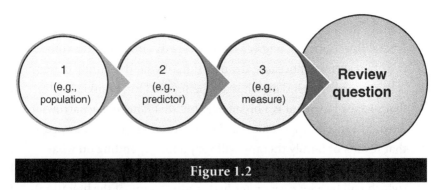

Figure 1.2

Specifying three elements of a review question.

understands what you are reviewing. Defining the topic is often not a trivial task, especially if the topic has been addressed in various research areas and disciplines. For example, the terms *personality* and *temperament* can mean very different things in the scientific psychological literature than they do in other research disciplines or the popular media. Chapter 4 introduces inclusion criteria, an important tool that will help you to define the scope and major terms and concepts. The review scope also clarifies what you are not reviewing, that is, it explains the boundaries of what you looked at in your literature review. You will see in Chapter 9 that clarifying what you have and have not reviewed is critical for literature reviews.

Exploring a Potential Topic

The review question and scope determine the sources you need to look at to answer the question (or questions). To design a manageable literature review for a well-defined topic, you need to know the characteristics of the literature base for the topic. So, before you start the actual literature review, get a sense of the existing literature. It is a good idea to do some exploratory searches: Look up the topic in sources of common knowledge such as Wikipedia for a broad overview, use sources such as Google Scholar to find popular articles, and skim recently published textbooks to get a feel for the research field. Although not part of the actual literature review, this process will help you to understand the breadth of the topic and the various aspects that researchers focus on.

Scoping out your topic will help you determine the sources you need to look at to answer the question. In other words, at what level should you review the literature? These days, you can choose from three possible levels:

- a review of individual research studies,
- a review of literature reviews, or
- a review of literature reviews summarizing literature reviews.

For a narrow review question, you can use individual research studies, that is, primary research literature. However, if your topic is popular, it makes sense to check for existing reviews. The quality of published literature reviews varies, but systematic reviews go to great lengths to identify relevant research on the topic and summarize it using a transparent approach. Systematic reviews and meta-analyses have clear reporting guidelines and tend to be structured similarly. Both types are useful in summarizing literature, so you could do a review of reviews. For very popular topics, there are even systematic reviews of systematic reviews, and you could use those for your own literature review (note that it doesn't get more "meta" than that, because you are summarizing reviews that themselves summarize reviews).

Regardless of what you decide, it is helpful to read existing reviews on a topic in which you are interested to get an idea of major themes and how the authors structure their arguments.

Breadth and Depth

It is important to carefully select the scope because you need to consider the breadth and the depth of a review. The scope should not be too broad (breadth), because you want your literature review to be as thorough (depth) as possible.

One way of dealing with too much literature is, of course, to look at only some of it. But to produce a valid and reliable research overview, you must be thorough and systematic in your search and selection of publications to review. Otherwise, the selection can be highly biased. With a biased selection, you may end up with an incorrect and misleading summary of the literature. It is important to be systematic in selecting material. This means that you do not choose only publications that you came across first or found the most interesting, ignoring other relevant literature. Also, you do not want to have so much literature that you are unable to review, let alone read, everything you have identified. The idea of a literature review is that you make something out of the material, that is, your synthesis of the literature is your unique contribution. A better approach to managing a lot of literature is to narrow your topic until you can achieve a balanced overview of what is out there.

Review Protocol

Before starting a literature review, consider writing a review protocol. A review protocol is a standard element in a systematic review, and the use of a protocol is a good idea for all literature reviews. A protocol is a plan for the review and a way to think through the content and methods in advance to ensure a solid and realistic product. PRISMA-P is a tool that helps authors write a systematic review protocol.

Helpful Resource

PRISMA-P (which stands for Preferred Reporting Items for Systematic Reviews and Meta-Analyses Protocols) is a checklist for review protocols. The tool can be accessed at http://www.prisma-statement. org/documents/PRISMA-P-checklist.pdf

Seventeen PRISMA-P items remind authors to specify the elements of the review, such as the literature sources, the inclusion criteria, and the data extraction plan. For example, one item is "Present draft of search strategy to be used for at least one electronic database, including planned limits, such that it could be repeated." Although the items are all geared toward a systematic review and/or meta-analysis, PRISMA-P is also helpful for other literature reviews because it provides a framework that helps you plan the review.

For your own review, it will help enormously to create a document that spells out the steps of the review methods you plan to use. This review protocol can serve as your to-do list for the review. In addition, when you are searching the literature or selecting publications, you will need to make a lot of decisions, and the review protocol can function as a working draft where you refine your methods and record interim results.

Cari's Caregiver Review

Cari has a literature review assignment on the role of informal caregivers. She realizes halfway through reading yet another article on the many settings and circumstances of informal caregiving that she is getting lost in the weeds of the literature. She decides she needs a plan for how to approach the literature review, and she puts together a document that outlines her review, that is, a review protocol. She lists the steps she plans to undertake and thinks through how she can best document the results of the review. She adds headings and subheadings to the protocol— for example, she has a paragraph clearly stating the objective of the review (see above), a section on the search strategy (see Chapter 3), and an outline of the results presentation including a draft evidence table (see Chapter 6). This preparation makes the review process much clearer, and breaking up the steps helps her to make it more manageable. She saves the original protocol (so that she has a record of it) and makes a copy of it to turn into her review report. Whenever she completes a step, she completes the respective section in the document until she has a finished report.

This plan can be as detailed or as elaborate as it needs to be. Likewise, reviews vary in how much information about the methods and procedures needs to be provided in your actual report. For example, if you are writing only a short introduction to a new research paper, the protocol or review plan will be equally short—and it may not need to be described in the body of the paper or included as an appendix. But if your literature is a stand-alone product, you can easily turn your protocol into the report of your literature review, building on it as though turning a pencil sketch into a colorful illustration. Chapter 9 discusses the various documentation options in detail.

CHAPTER 1 ACTION STEPS

- ☐ Identify the type of literature review you are writing (a stand-alone product, a part of a research report, a short background section to frame new research).
- ☐ Specify how long the review needs to be, what sections it needs to include, and any other instructions.
- ☐ Scope the possible topic by exploring the literature and learning about important issues in the field.
- ☐ Formulate a review question or review objective.
- ☐ Consider using a review protocol to plan the review and to follow for the remainder of the review project.

2

Where to Look: Choosing Databases and Other Sources of Literature

This chapter shows you what sources to use in your literature review and different approaches to finding scientific information. It introduces many options and will help you make informed decisions about which are the best sources for your own literature review and how to get the most out of them.

> Going back to our cooking analogy, the "where to look" stage is the equivalent of finding the best shops for the ingredients you need. Depending on your budget, the amount of time you have to prepare, and how elaborate your dinner is going to be, you might get your ingredients at the corner shop, or you may need to head to the specialty delicatessen out of town.

http://dx.doi.org/10.1037/0000155-003
Conducting Your Literature Review, by S. Hempel

Systematic reviews that strive for comprehensiveness will often use all of the sources listed in Exhibit 2.1 and use multiple strategies within the categories (e.g., search multiple research databases). For your literature review you need to decide which and how many sources you want to use. To do this, you need to take into account the following:

- availability and accessibility of sources;
- relevance of the literature included in each source to your topic and review question;
- research volume and whether your topic is well-established or new/unique;
- your own resources, such as time and energy; and
- your goals, your audience, and format of the review.

Availability is particularly an issue for research databases. You will see that some databases are publicly available, whereas others require a subscription. Some sources are more relevant to specific topics than others, as you will see in the discussion about gray literature. If you are researching a topic that has not received much research attention, or if you are interested in a unique aspect, you may need to go through half a dozen sources to find information. On the other hand,

---

Exhibit 2.1

Sources and Strategies to Identify Research Literature

- Research databases
- Gray literature
- Hand search
- Reference-mining
- Related articles
- Forward search
- Citation report
- Content experts
- Books and book chapters

---

more well-established areas with large research volumes may yield more information in one database than you can cope with.

But the goal of your literature review will be your key consideration when choosing how many sources and strategies you should employ. The search effort should be proportionate to the type of literature review you are planning to write (see Figure 1.1). If you are writing a stand-alone review, you should expect to spend many hours exploring sources. For your thesis, you might expend up to half your efforts on the literature review and the rest on your original study design, execution, and reporting. But for a brief review that serves as an introduction section for an article, you would want to dedicate the bulk of your time to developing the main idea or explaining the experiment and describing/interpreting results, so the effort spent on the literature review would be less, relatively speaking.

As a general rule, it is a good idea to use two different sources of information for your literature review project. Those can be two research databases, a database search and reference-mining, or a database and gray literature. Different sources have different advantages and shortcomings, and if used together they will make a more complete basis for your literature review. Using different sources protects against *selection bias* (i.e., having a sample of literature that is not a good representation of the existing literature base).

ROLE OF THE LIBRARY

Throughout this chapter, I refer to "your library." Your university library in particular is a key partner for literature reviews. Many libraries provide advice on literature reviews on their websites and have assembled resource collections for popular topics. Many librarians are trained information specialists with extensive expertise in scholarly information sources. Libraries subscribe to research databases and can obtain articles or books through interlibrary loans even when they do not have access to a resource themselves. Now is a good time to familiarize yourself with your library. You will soon become a power user, as you get more efficient and begin to reap multiple benefits from all of the library's resources.

RESEARCH DATABASES

Whether you are writing a background section for a research publication or are working on a full literature review, the kind of information you will summarize is primarily research literature that is published in scientific journals. Several databases index research literature to help you to retrieve relevant information. For example, these databases include information about all articles that have been published in an issue of a scientific journal. Among the many prominent research databases that are portals to a wealth of information are the following:

- **PsycINFO**, which is dedicated to the psychological scientific literature, includes more than 3 million records. Maintained by the American Psychological Association, it indexes journal articles, book chapters, books, and dissertations relevant to behavioral science and mental health. The database indexes research going backward (it now includes studies that were published 120 years ago) and forward (weekly updates capture the latest research on a topic).
- One of the best-maintained databases is **PubMed**, which everyone can access for free through the U.S. National Library of Medicine, National Institutes of Health. It includes more than 29 million biomedical literature citations and has broad coverage, including numerous psychology journals. You can search it on your computer or your smartphone.
- Depending on your literature review topic, you may also want to search **CINAHL**, which includes research in nursing and allied health professions.
- **ERIC** is a database dedicated to research in education that is funded by the U.S. Department of Education.
- **Sociological Abstracts** covers more than 50 years of sociology research to date.
- Economy, business, and finance research articles are included in the database **EconLit**.

- The **Web of Science** covers a broad spectrum of scientific journals. It also indexes conference abstracts (see the Gray Literature section) and provides additional literature review functions such as a citation report (see Finding the Most-Cited Articles).

These are just a handful of the hundreds of databases out there. Check which ones you can access through your university library or library account. See if the library maintains a list of research databases that you can browse online, or ask a librarian about the available resources and what they recommend for your topic.

Helpful Resource

PubMed can be accessed for free through the U.S. National Library of Medicine at the National Institutes of Health and includes more than 29 million biomedical citations. Visit https://www.ncbi.nlm. nih.gov/pubmed

Databases vary in their range, accessibility, and user-friendliness. The database range is defined by the content and research areas covered, by the type of indexed information (e.g., citations vs. searchable, full-text articles), by how far back the databases go, and how well they are maintained (e.g., someone needs to add new material daily to keep them current). Some databases are freely accessible online; for others, you depend on your university to have a subscription to the database. Databases also vary in their search functionality. The search platform that hosts the database will determine the format and syntax being used for the searches. Some databases are menu-based, user-friendly, and designed to assist a range of users, whereas others require detailed knowledge of the syntax and how search terms can be manipulated to retrieve results. Hence, depending on the platform, the database, and the complexity of search strings, some searches are better designed and executed by trained information specialists, such as librarians.

Related Articles

Several research databases offer a *related article* function, that is, they identify citations that are similar. This function is particularly useful when you have come across a publication that is exactly what you are looking for. In that case, you are using the publication you really like as a "seed article" to find similar publications.

In some other cases, you may have identified an author or author group who have published a couple of important articles in your research area. It might be worth finding more articles by the author because there is a good chance that the author has published extensively on the topic and that you will find more relevant publications that way. Here you are using the author, not a particular publication, as the seed.

Forward Search

Another useful feature of databases is the *forward search* function. A forward search finds publications that have referenced a publication of interest (i.e., it looks for publications that have cited a publication that you know is relevant for your review). This type of search can be done in the database Web of Science (subscription-based) and in the search engine Google Scholar (open access), for example. Authors of publications that cite an article of interest are likely to work in a similar research field, so these other articles are worth checking out. A forward search is another way to increase the odds of finding relevant publications.

GRAY LITERATURE

Not all pertinent research information is published as an article in a peer-reviewed scientific journal. Information from other sources is referred to as *gray* (or *grey*) *literature* and includes, for example, government reports or web content and documents from professional organizations such as the American Psychological Association. Gray literature includes research information that is public (e.g., if you search the organization's website, you'll find it and can access it) but not published in a traditional research journal format. Whether to include gray literature in your literature review is not an easy decision.

First, there is the issue of how to go about finding gray literature. Your favorite search engine may produce tens of thousands of links for a topic. For your literature review, the sheer number is problematic because you would not be able to look at them all unless you had infinite time. So you would need to come up with an arbitrary cutoff. That is, you would have to say that after page 10 or so of search results, you quit following the links. Another big problem is that the searches cannot be replicated. When you use a search engine to search for a topic, there is no guarantee that someone else will get the same result. In fact, there is no guarantee that you will get the same result if you do the same search 5 minutes later. Not only is new content constantly added and indexed in search engines, but Google, for example, also tailors search results to your location (whether through location tracking on your mobile device or by IP address), so if your location changes, the results might as well. Similarly, your search history alters the relevance ranking of search results. This lack of reproducibility is problematic because a literature review aims to be objective and replicable.

File Drawer Problem

There is also some debate about what is or what counts as gray literature. Some gray literature is very useful and rather important. Conference abstracts are often included in gray literature, for example. This type of research information is interesting for two reasons. First, not all research studies get published; this is known as the *file drawer problem*. Many researchers have a bunch of unpublished data and unfinished manuscripts in their possession that they may never get around to publishing in a journal article—these data and unfinished manuscripts are sitting in a file drawer in their office or, more likely, an electronic file on their computer. But these authors may have presented the data at a conference, which is a lot less work than formal publishing, and their abstract would have been included in conference proceedings.

Conference abstracts are often published before a full publication, so they can be said to represent the latest research at the time of a literature review. Thus, including conference abstracts can help you write an up-to-date literature review on the topic. On the other hand, peer review for scientific journal submissions serves as a quality check, and many times, problems with the data and their interpretation are discovered and corrected during the peer review process. Furthermore, the limited information available in abbreviated formats such as conference abstracts may be seriously misleading when summarizing research results. Also, conference abstracts often need to be manually searched (see the Hand Search section), so you would need to know that a conference of interest was held and then search the proceedings for relevant research. This takes time and may not be worth the effort.

Another source is registries for research studies. In recent years, it has become more common (and is required for some research studies) to register research studies, including systematic reviews. Example registries are http://www.clinicaltrials.gov for U.S. research trials or PROSPERO (https://www.crd.york.ac.uk/prospero/) for systematic reviews. Primarily, these registries are used to identify studies but some registries also contain the results of the research.

One final consideration with gray literature versus peer-reviewed is that research with interesting results, in particular, statistically significant results, is more likely to get published as a journal article. The phenomenon of selectively publishing some research results but not others is known as *publication bias*. This type of reporting bias is problematic when you are trying to summarize a research field. For an objective summary, you want to present the available research, but when you restrict yourself to research published in scientific journals, you are more likely to find statistically significant results. Including gray literature will provide a more complete picture of the research base. However, keep in mind that there is no guarantee that research is even presented at conferences— some potentially relevant work may never see the light of day in any form.

HAND SEARCH

Hand searching describes a process in which you do not rely on an electronic search in a database but instead manually search for literature. This can mean screening tables of contents of journals to find relevant articles because you suspect that the article was not indexed correctly or could not

Mia's Motivational Interviewing Review

Mia is working on a literature review on motivational interviewing as applied in schools. She searches research databases, including ERIC, to identify relevant scientific literature. Because she primarily wants to find out whether and in what capacity motivational interviewing is used in schools, she plans to review websites of large school districts for any reference to motivational interviewing. However, faced with thousands of school districts, Mia first finds the 10 largest school districts in the country and then searches their websites one by one. That way she keeps the gray literature search more systematic, transparent, and manageable.

be captured with your search strategy. As you can imagine, this process is very tedious, even when you are restricting it to the most relevant journals. In some cases, hand searching cannot be avoided. Conference proceedings may not be indexed electronically and may need to be hand searched: sometimes databases may have indexed a conference but not at the individual contribution level (i.e., you may find an entry about the conference that does not mention which topics were presented at the conference).

REFERENCE-MINING

Reference-mining is also a key method for identifying relevant publications. *Reference-mining* describes the process of screening the bibliographies of pertinent literature reviews on the topic, as well as screening the citations of publications that you have selected for your literature review. As outlined in Chapter 1, it is always a good idea to find published reviews on the topic that you are planning to review. The reviewers may have organized their material in an evidence table, which will give you a lot of information about possibly relevant studies (see Chapter 8 for more about evidence tables). With individual articles, you need to screen the introduction and discussion section to locate citations. Reference-mining takes advantage of the fact that other authors have already researched the topic. These authors not only have found important research but often also provide valuable information about the research studies. This information will help you further to decide whether a citation is likely to be relevant. Hence, reference-mining is an effective and convenient search strategy.

FINDING THE MOST-CITED ARTICLES

Another strategy you should consider for your review is finding the most-cited articles for the research area you are summarizing. A "citation report" function is included in the Web of Science. A citation report identifies the top-cited articles in a research area. The top five or top 10 publications cited in a particular research area are central resources. For a brief literature review, you may not even need to explore the field further after identifying these.

Google Scholar also ranks publications and provides an estimate of how many times an article has been cited. The advanced search box lets you calibrate searches, such as by specifying the date range or exact phrases. A key advantage of Google Scholar is that it searches full-text publications, not just citations. In Chapter 3 you will see how most databases let you search the title, abstract, keywords, and other citation information but not the full text of the article; Google Scholar is one of the few exceptions. However, a Google Scholar search cannot be replicated

Helpful Resource

Google Scholar provides access to published scientific journal articles as well as other publicly available research material. It can be accessed for free at https://scholar.google.com

because the search algorithm is not transparent, and the website's content and functionality are continuously being updated.

GETTING INPUT FROM CONTENT EXPERTS

A key source of information for literature reviews is people with expertise on the topic. You might know someone at your university who has published on the topic, or your supervisor may have input. You could ask them to review your sources (e.g., for advice on databases), skim your identified literature to make sure that you have not missed anything critical, or suggest key articles to get started.

Contacting authors who have published on the topic, to ask them about published or unpublished data, is also a search strategy for literature reviews. But to do this systematically (i.e., as a proper search strategy), you need to invest time and effort. You need to be able to document who was contacted and what your criterion for selecting experts was. You need to find contact details and set up a tracking and reminder system for authors who don't reply (e.g., up to two reminders with 1-week intervals in between e-mails).

In both cases, be mindful that researchers are busy and will need some time even if they want to help. You may not get a response if you do not know the expert personally, but in any case, make sure that you ask early enough (as the adage goes, "procrastination on your part does not constitute an emergency on my part," and you should assume most subject matter experts feel this way). For other input from content experts in literature reviews (e.g., experts serving as key informants or a technical expert panel supporting a review) check out the literature on scoping reviews and systematic reviews listed in the Further Reading section.

BOOKS AND BOOK CHAPTERS

For some topics, you may find textbooks covering the topic or books dedicated to your review question. These are invaluable sources of overview information and key articles. However, with books, it is important to check how recent the citations are. Also keep in mind that the citations may only be examples that underpin points that the author is trying to

Emilia's Extraversion Review

Emilia wants to review the validity of extraversion measures as part of her thesis. A scoping exercise showed her which psychologists have worked on the construct of extraversion, and from that she has a set of search terms for extraversion and personality trait systems that she can use. She knows that the most important database for this topic will be PsycINFO, but she will also search PubMed to look for biomedical literature. In addition, she will reference-mine publications that met her inclusion criteria, that is, scan the introduction, discussion, and bibliography of the publications, thus taking advantage of other authors' work who are likely to have cited important studies. Finally, because this topic is so specific, she plans to run the reference list by a content expert at her university to make sure that she has all the relevant studies she needs to write the review. She realizes that this plan is ambitious because it involves multiple sources and a sequential approach (she needs to complete her searches first before she has something to show to the expert). Hence, she makes sure to get the searches started several months before the thesis is due.

make, rather than a complete and systematic listing of the available literature such as you would find in a recently published systematic review in a journal article.

WHICH SOURCES AND HOW MANY?

Now that you have seen all the possible ways of identifying material for your literature review, how can you decide which sources to use and how many? You should use more than one source, as mentioned in the beginning of this chapter. But keep in mind that each search takes time and effort, and the material you locate may be too much to deal with in your timeframe, with your available resources. For assistance with the decision, go back to the criteria mentioned in the beginning of the chapter: availability, relevance, research volume, your resources, and your goals.

For many literature review projects, it is appropriate to combine a database search and reference-mining. You can search only what is available to you, but it is critical that you search the most appropriate database that you have access to. If you are not sure, ask your professor or a librarian for guidance.

Whether you need other sources, and which other sources you need, depend on your topic and your review. Scoping out the topic, as described in Chapter 1, is critical. Different sources have different purposes and different advantages. For example, if you are reviewing a fast-moving research field, you probably need to search conference abstracts.

We know that some strategies are more effective than others; for example, reference-mining for pertinent articles tends to locate a lot of relevant literature, whereas hand searches may feel like looking for a needle in a haystack. But if you are reviewing an obscure topic, you may need to employ lots of sources to get information. At the very least, you need to be able to show that you looked in multiple sources, even if you didn't find anything.

The effort you dedicate to the searches needs to be proportionate to the type of literature review you are undertaking. Also, it is more important to apply a search strategy systematically in key sources rather than search multiple and diverse sources in a more haphazard way.

SOURCE DOCUMENTATION

It is important that you list the sources you used to find the material for your literature review; that is, you should be able to say which sources you searched and when. This is important for your own records. As noted in the introduction to this book, reviewing literature can be an iterative process, so going back to searches once or more is something you should expect. A list of sources is also important from a scientific point of view so that your literature review results can be replicated. Finally, information on the sources and search dates will give the reader of your literature review an idea of what type of material you included.

CHAPTER 2 ACTION STEPS

☐ Check out which research databases you have access to (e.g., PsycINFO, PsycARTICLES) and/or that are publicly available (e.g., PubMed, Google Scholar).

☐ Select one or two databases for your literature search that index research relevant to your topic.

☐ Consider reference-mining, that is, screening the bibliographies of relevant studies for additional material for your review.

☐ Check the other sources mentioned in this chapter to see if any are useful and feasible for your project (e.g., gray literature, citation report).

☐ Review your timeline for the literature review and check your plan for feasibility.

How to Look:
Developing Search Strategies

This chapter is all about how to look for material that you can include in your review. It first invites you to think about how to translate the components of your review question into search terms. Then it explains how to develop search strategies for electronic databases and search engines.

Coming back to the cooking analogy, you've identified the stores where you want to shop, and now you are shopping for the right ingredients in each of those places.

http://dx.doi.org/10.1037/0000155-004
Conducting Your Literature Review, by S. Hempel

SEARCH STRUCTURE

A detailed review question can be easily translated into a search strategy. The strategy will define the main components of the publications that should be reviewed. But first, it is useful to structure the components of the review question into a search framework.

The framework should address the key elements that are included in the review question, such as the study population or target the publication should address (e.g., psychology students), the outcomes and measures (e.g., what was assessed), and the intervention or exposure (e.g., the independent variable). Think of the search strategy as a Venn diagram as illustrated in Figure 3.1. The search strategy aims to identify the center of the Venn diagram, that is, publications that address all three of the components included in this example.

Your search will be reflective of the review question, but you also need to think about types of publications (which are discussed in Chapter 4). For example, you may be interested only in existing reviews or only in experimental studies. Searching is often an iterative process, and once you are familiar with Chapter 4, you are likely to add another component to your Venn diagram.

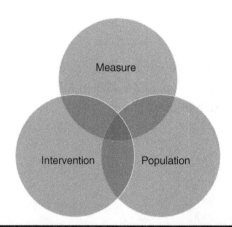

Figure 3.1

Venn diagram for literature searches.

Search Terms

To compose the search strategy, you need to come up with search terms. To avoid getting caught in a tangle, it is best to come up with search terms for each review component separately. Although your search will combine all components, it is important to develop each component separately. For example, you may have a set of terms listing all the outcomes you are interested in, a set of synonyms for the intervention you are looking for, and a set of terms that describe the population you want to study.

In the process of coming up with search terms, it is really helpful to brainstorm synonyms. For example, you may want to review the *harms* and *benefits* of an intervention. Some databases search for certain synonyms automatically, but not all do this, and databases do not necessarily do this systematically. Hence it is important to search not just for the word *harm* but also for terms such as *adverse event, adverse effect, safety, health risk*, or *side effect*.

Searching for *benefits* is even more difficult because study authors will have reported on individual results and outcome measures, and even when they saw a benefit, the citation is not likely to describe the effect as a *benefit*. For example, the authors might write, "Depression scores were improved in the intervention group." It is obvious that this is a benefit—so obvious that the authors do not explicitly say this or use the word *benefit*.

To generate good search results in a case like this, it is critical to use the types of measures and outcome domains that study authors may have investigated and supplement with general terms such as *effect, effectiveness*, or *improve* that could describe the information you are looking for. Scoping out the research field and conducting some exploratory searches will help you anticipate how researchers and database staff may have labeled the topic of interest. Terminology often varies by research discipline, so it is useful to find a couple of examples from each one if you are working on an interdisciplinary topic.

Some terms, on the other hand, are not useful because they may be relevant in too many contexts (e.g., *fall*, as in "fall prevention in nursing homes" or "numbers expected to fall" or even "experience of depression during fall and winter"). Depending on how common the term is, you may need to avoid it altogether or combine it with other search terms that narrow down the context. In addition, each term should be assessed for its incremental validity, that is, whether and how many additional citations will be found by adding the term. An example is the term *depression level*, which will not find any additional citations if the term *depression* is already part of the search strategy (the term *depression level* here doesn't add anything if *depression* is already present).

Boolean Operators

Search strings combine terms with Boolean logic (*AND*, *OR*, *NOT*). As a general rule, *AND* will reduce the number of search hits because it means that two terms are required to be present in the citation. *OR*, on the other hand, will increase the number of hits because either one or the other term can be present. Two different components of the topic should be combined with the operator *AND* (e.g., sample population and the independent variable of interest), whereas synonyms within a component need an *OR* (e.g., *psychology students* OR *students of psychology*). In some cases, it will be possible to use *NOT* to exclude some terms or term combinations because you know they are irrelevant (e.g., *NOT animals* when you are interested in only human participants and are sure that the publications you want would not mention animals for any other reason than describing their sample). Apart from standard operators, databases usually have a wildcard option, that is, a signal to automatically search all variations of a term. For example, *improv** searches for the word stem and will retrieve all records that include words that start with *improv-*, including *improve, improved, improving, improvement,* and *improvements.*

Many databases let users search for an exact phrase (e.g., "fall prevention"). Searching without the quotes will retrieve all citations that have any of the individual words in the citation record somewhere (e.g., "rates were expected to *fall*" in the abstract and "Journal of Psychological

Prevention" in the journal title). Some databases offer additional functions such as the *near function*, a function that specifies word proximity (e.g., the words need to be within three words of each other). For example, if you search for *psychology adj2 students* in the database MEDLINE, it will search all combinations of *psychology* and *students* that are adjacent to each other. The number indicates how many words you allow to come between your search terms—in this case, two. This expression will find all combinations of phrases that have the words *psychology* and *students* in close proximity (e.g., "psychology students," "students of psychology," "students in psychology").

Generally, the search strategy should operationalize the review question. In other words, the search strategy should translate the concepts of the review questions into search terms. However, some aspects of the review may not be operationalizable in the search strategy. For example, the topic of the review may be long-term effects of a behavior or procedure, but the timing of the measurements is often not reported in the title or abstract of the publication. In most databases, search algorithms use the citation, abstract, and keywords to select relevant publications. When an aspect is unlikely to be mentioned at this level, ANDing it (i.e., requiring that the term is present in the record) will exclude many relevant studies. For example, a search using the word *long-term* would exclude studies that report on the timing of the outcome assessment only in the full text of the publication as well as studies that did not use the specific term "long-term" but specified the follow-up duration or assessment date (e.g., "10-year follow-up").

Indexing Terms

Many databases carefully index citations and use controlled vocabulary to document the citations. For example, PsycINFO uses the *Thesaurus of Psychological Index Terms* and PubMed uses Medical Subject Headings (MeSH) to help database users find relevant publications. These descriptors have been added by database staff (a process called *indexing*) to help find studies, and these *tags* are very useful for literature searches. These terms and the term hierarchy are often a searchable part of the database and can help identify the right search terms for a topic. But a key limitation of relying on indexed terms is that it takes databases a while to fully index citations. Hence, if a search strategy relies entirely on assigned keywords, it will miss the newest research on the topic because the most recent citations will not have been tagged yet.

Search Filters

Throughout, it will require some thought to translate your review scope and inclusion criteria into a search strategy. Your complete search strategy (using Boolean operators, indexing terms, etc.) will function as a search filter to identify those studies you are most interested in.

Databases have a variety of *limiters* that can be used by database users; for example, searches can be restricted to a period of publication years or certain publication languages. The impact of limiters varies considerably. For example, restricting to a specific (searchable) study design will greatly reduce the search yield. Restricting the search date to newer literature, however, can be easily achieved, but its effects will be less pronounced because more research has been published in recent years. Nonetheless, restricting to specific search dates can be useful, in particular, when there is a rationale for it. An example is research that is embedded in context; the environment may be changed due to technological advances or other factors, making it difficult to compare the results of research assessing technologies that was published decades ago.

Databases will have some filters that are ready to use; for example, PsycINFO tags the methodology of publications so that you can easily identify certain types of studies. Limiting searches to publications that report on research based on a particular study design (e.g., experiments) can make literature searches much more manageable. But keep in mind that some aspects of research studies are better indexed than are others. For example, a number of search filters exist for randomized controlled trials, a popular medical research design. This is in part because there has been a lot of research dedicated to identifying trials, and research authors are used to labeling their trials as a randomized controlled trial so that they can be recognized as such and found in electronic searches. For other aspects of research articles, including other study designs, search filters are less reliable. Databases as well as associations of librarians such as The InterTASC Information Specialists' Sub-Group have collated search filters for different study designs, types of data, and databases.

Helpful Resource

The InterTASC Information Specialists' Sub-Group (https://sites. google.com/a/york.ac.uk/issg-search-filters-resource) has collated a large number of search filters for different databases.

For other aspects, you may be able to design a filter yourself. For example, if you want to limit the review to U.S. settings, you need to explore whether and how this can be operationalized in the database (e.g., by using the first author's affiliation as a proxy). Many databases have a collection of "canned searches," that is, search filters that someone has developed to identify a particular type of citation (e.g., gene therapy trials) and that the database saved for others to use. Check out the tool section of the database or ask a librarian.

SEARCHING CITATIONS VERSUS SEARCHING PUBLICATIONS

Before you start searching, determine the format of the material in the research database. Note that most databases let you search only the citation rather than the full-text publication. That means your search filters are designed for an abbreviated version of the publication, that is, a very short summary. For your literature review you are of course interested in the full text (i.e., the entire article), but what you can search in most electronic databases is the title, the abstract (100–230 words max), the keywords assigned by database staff, and the full reference (e.g., journal, volume).

As you can imagine, the fact that you are searching a summary rather than the full text of the scientific publication can be problematic. For some topics it is simply unfortunate that you do not have access to the full text because you will not know from the abbreviated format whether what you are looking for is included in the full text of the publication. Say you are looking for whether mini pigs make good emotional support animals. You may have to keep your search broad and look for *animals* and *pigs* because the type of animal may not be specified in the title or abstract of the publication.

For other topics, searching citations for a particular term can actually introduce selection bias (i.e., distort your search yield). Think about a situation in which you are trying to establish whether there is a difference between two subpopulations (e.g., gender differences in response to alcohol treatment). Directly searching for the effect (e.g., gender differences) that you are trying to find out about increases the chance of finding primarily studies with positive, affirmative results. The reason is that the authors will have highlighted the positive finding in the title or abstract of the publication. In other words, because they found a gender effect in response to alcohol treatment, they mentioned it in the summary. On the other hand, all the studies that did not find gender differences in response to alcohol treatment may not point that out in the title or abstract of their publication. Instead, these authors will have concentrated on other findings (e.g., the size of the treatment effect or other moderator effects). It does not mean that these authors did not test for gender effects. They just did not highlight the absence of gender differences because authors tend to report only the interesting bits in this synopsis. With this in mind, you have two options: Either leave out the effect that you are most interested in, or use only databases that search the full text of publications. In our example, leaving out the term you are most interested in would mean not using the term *gender differences* at all and instead searching for *alcohol treatment* only. That way you would get to a representative sample of studies that you can then search to determine whether there is a lot of evidence for gender differences or not.

Fortunately, a few databases let you search the full text of the publication, not just the citation. This includes PsycARTICLES, a database of psychological articles that are searchable as full text, and the Google Scholar Web search engine. Searching the full text of publications is very convenient because you do not have to depend on the information authors highlighted in the title or abstract of publications.

SEARCH STRATEGY DOCUMENTATION

The same principle about documentation that was mentioned in the previous chapter applies here as well: How you went about your search, including what search terms you typed into databases (and when you typed them), should be clearly reported. You should be able to communicate whether you found the material for your searches in a general database search (using which search terms), which filters were applied (and where they came from), and whether you used the forward search and/or a related article function (and for which article and for how many articles you followed up on). The idea is that the process can, at least in theory, be replicated, that is, someone else should be able to enter the same terms and get the same results.

Documenting the search strategy will help you remember what you have already covered in your search; it will make it much easier to make any revisions; and, as a scientific method, this documentation allows the process to be replicable. Although some people say that designing a search strategy is more of an art than a science, you may have gleaned from the information presented here that designing a search strategy is complex. Having a clearly structured and well-documented search strategy will make the process transparent and will also help you to move through your strategy smoothly. It can get messy; many systematic reviewers have their strategy peer-reviewed because it can get so complicated.

The search strategy is also useful information for the reader of the review. So, for literature review projects it is a good idea to document the actual search strategy (the exact search strings) for each searched database. Of note, in systematic reviews, a search strategy has to be documented in full for at least one database, and many journals will publish the search

Quinn's Quality of Life in the Workplace Review

Quinn works on a research project assessing how the workplace affects quality of life. Part of his thesis is a literature review. Quinn sees after his first attempt that he cannot just type *quality of life* in the research databases he is searching because it brings up all sorts of citations that mention *life* and *quality* somewhere in the citation record but that have nothing to do with quality of life. Instead, he searches for the exact phrase by putting *quality of life* in quotation marks to narrow his search. He also notices that he is not capturing publications that address the same construct but don't say the exact phrase "quality of life." He adds some synonyms ("quality of life" OR "well-being" OR "wellbeing" OR "well being" OR "life quality") to capture these studies. But he also looks up common measures of quality of life and adds the titles or abbreviations of the tests (e.g., SF36), and that addition makes all the difference. This search finds studies that clearly have measured quality of life. Using this combination strategy, he increases the sensitivity of the search (i.e., a high number of relevant citations) without compromising specificity (i.e., having to go through hundreds of irrelevant citations). He adds *OR* between the quality-of-life terms and between the workplace terms to capture his review topic. He makes sure to copy the entire search string—("quality of life" OR "well-being" OR "wellbeing" OR "well being" OR "life quality" OR SF36 OR QOLS OR WHOQOL) AND ("work place" OR staff OR worker OR employ* OR profession* OR office)—into the appendix of his review write-up so that he can communicate how and what exactly he searched for. He states the database he used and the date he ran the search, and he adds that he used two database filters (Review, to find secondary literature on the topic, and English Language).

strategy together with the results of the review. In addition, the dates of the searches need to be recorded. Research continues to be published, and it is important to convey the latest date on which you reviewed the published literature. This information will also help the reader decide whether you missed a recent relevant study that is not included in your review or the publication came out after your literature searches were complete. To document the full search strategy, you need to copy the search strings from the research database. In some cases, databases will let the user download the full search string with the search results in a convenient export format so that you can put it straight into the appendix of your review write-up.

RECALL, RETRIEVAL, AND YIELD

The purpose of developing a search strategy is to identify the pool of relevant citations on the topic. The quality of searches can be formally evaluated by *recall* and *retrieval* rates. Recall rates describe how many relevant citations are included in the search output; retrieval rates describe how many citations known to be relevant have been successfully retrieved through the searches. All search strategies need to consider the trade-off between *sensitivity* (recall; successfully identifying relevant studies) and *specificity* (precision; successfully excluding irrelevant citations). An inclusive search strategy will identify more relevant studies but at the expense of also including many irrelevant citations. A formal evaluation of a search strategy is a separate research project, but your search strategy should have at least *face validity*. A search has face validity when it uses search terms that a reader who is familiar with the research area expects, the terms are sufficiently broad to cover the review scope, and the search terms are combined in a logical and transparent way.

Finally, the total *yield* of the search is also important. The search yield describes the number of citations retrieved by the search strategy (*hits*) and, depending on the research volume and specificity of the topic, can range from a handful to tens of thousands of citations. Sometimes the yield may simply be too large for the available time and resources that it will take to screen it all, in which case you need to revise your search strategy. However, remember that the search yield is not the material pool you will work with for the review. There are two more steps involved in identifying the material that will be included in the literature review. These are laid out in Chapter 4.

CHAPTER 3 ACTION STEPS

- ☐ Put a Venn diagram together to depict the different search term categories and concepts defining the search.
- ☐ Look up the Boolean operators to combine search terms in the database you are searching.
- ☐ Familiarize yourself with index terms used in the database.
- ☐ Design your search filter, that is, your search strategy, to select citations of interest.
- ☐ Check the search yield (number of search hits) and decide whether you have enough information and can cope with the yield.
- ☐ Consider reviewing the search recall (Is there a large number of relevant citations in your search output?) and the search retrieval rate (Did a relevant article that you know about come up in your search output?).

What to Look For:
Deciding What Literature
to Include

Your literature searches will find all sorts of literature and types of publications. Once you have generated lists of search results, you need to broadly categorize the research literature. This chapter explains what to look for once you have completed the first literature searches. It introduces the concept of eligibility criteria and describes the inclusion screening process.

> At this point in our cooking adventure, we are now identifying the ingredients we'll need from each store.

http://dx.doi.org/10.1037/0000155-005
Conducting Your Literature Review, by S. Hempel

TYPES OF PUBLICATIONS

At this point of the process, you need to decide what you want to summarize in your literature review. This decision shapes what you are looking for, in terms of both the content that makes the material relevant and the type of publication that you get the information from. In most cases, a literature review summarizes the results of scientific research. But scientific research can be found in many different types of publications, so first you want to look at the existing publications very broadly. Think about the level (e.g., primary or secondary research), the type of information (e.g., empirical data or opinion papers), and methodological approach (e.g., quantitative or qualitative research).

Level

As discussed in Chapter 1, literature reviews may summarize original research or other publication types, including other reviews. An example of a review summarizing secondary literature is a systematic review of systematic reviews. Because the numbers of publications in general and reviews specifically have dramatically increased in recent years, you first need to decide what you want to summarize: primary or secondary literature or a mixture of both. This depends on what exactly you are looking for, that is, the question that you want to answer with the available literature. And of course, it also depends on whether already-existing secondary literature has addressed the topic you are interested in.

If there are literature reviews on the topic, you might want to summarize these. The existing reviews probably approach the topic from different angles rather than provide the same information. It is also possible that your review question is either narrower than the published reviews, in which case you would extract the information you want from the existing literature, or broader, in which case you can combine the information and integrate it in your review. If your topic is meditation, there is an enormous amount of primary research out there, and it is more efficient to summarize secondary literature in your review if you want to answer a general question, such as the effects of meditation on coping with chronic pain.

Other topics may not have been addressed yet in secondary literature, or there may be only a couple of reviews out there; in the latter case,
it does not make sense to summarize such a small number of reviews.
Another common occurrence is published literature reviews that are
outdated. It is difficult to decide when a literature review is outdated, but
if the search is more than a decade old (or more than a couple of years
old in a rapidly developing field), you can assume that there is more
new research out there that is probably worth summarizing. Although
it is true that not all new research challenges the conclusions of existing
literature reviews—research is just as likely to substantiate what we know
with more data—you almost need to complete the review first before
you know for sure. In addition, in some cases the subject of your review
may develop as well (e.g., technology to support clinical care)—another
reason why the published literature reviews may be outdated.

 Terrence's Telehealth Review

Terrence is interested in the effectiveness of Internet-delivered
cognitive behavior therapy (iCBT). He knows that this kind of
telehealth application is a fast-moving field, and because of this fast-
moving nature, the published reviews are often out of date. Hence,
he decides to summarize primary research studies published in the
past 3 years. He selects one clinical condition (e.g., anxiety) and
one setting (e.g., U.S. applications) to keep the review manageable
and the studies comparable. He keeps track of published literature
reviews that he comes across by putting them in a stack for "background papers," then he works them into the introduction of his
review. He cites reviews to indicate how common iCBT has become,
what iCBT looks like and how it is defined, and the challenges of
implementing it in healthcare systems, thereby putting a very nice
introduction together.

Again, a scoping exercise to explore the topic and the initial search yield will help you decide the type of publication to use. But regardless of the level of research literature selected for the review, it is always a good idea to look up existing reviews. The reviews will help you understand the breadth of the topic, research dilemmas and controversies, and how others have attempted to structure and summarize the topic.

Type of Information

Another very broad characteristic of a scientific publication is whether the author reports empirical data or expresses their opinion or take on an issue. Basically, you want to evaluate whether a paper is a write-up of a research study or another type of scientific publication. Often, it is easier to restrict yourself to empirical studies for your literature review. You can keep opinion papers as background papers if they resonate with you, but it is important that you recognize this broad differentiation (see Chapter 5 for more about organizing your material). Of course, for some topics you will need to look for scientific publications that are not empirical studies. In particular, if you are reviewing the literature for a new topic, such as to what extent gene editing can be used to increase people's intelligence, you will find information primarily in theoretical papers.

Methodological Approach

This feature is the most complicated because there are many different study designs and methodological approaches, there is no agreed-upon nomenclature, and the terminology varies by discipline, so it is difficult even to recognize methodological study categories. And you need to think about determining the best methodological approach for the question you are working to answer and its research field. Research disciplines differentiate a variety of research method categories. For example, the biomedical literature broadly categorizes empirical literature into experimental and observational studies (in experimental studies, an investigator manipulates an independent variable and studies the effects; in observational studies, a researcher observes effects, and the independent variable is not under the control of the investigator). Psychologists usually focus more on the sophistication of the analytic method rather than the basic study design. The differentiation between quantitative and qualitative data is also considered critical in some research areas.

Before you start your literature review, it is a good idea to look up study designs, such as by using course material or consulting research methods books (e.g., Shadish, Cook, & Campbell, 2001, or Urban & Van Eeden-Moorefield, 2018, in this book series; see the Further Reading section). Remind yourself of the different methodological approaches in the research field that you are studying—this is part of scoping out the literature, as described in Chapter 1. Then determine the best study design, data type, and analytic method for your review question. Some researchers do this by asking themselves, "If resources were unlimited, how would I design a study that answers the question I have?" Identifying the best primary research designs for literature review questions is difficult. It may be worth asking someone who knows, that is, a subject matter expert, if you are not sure (see Chapter 2 for tips on approaching subject matter experts). If a certain study design or analysis method is recommended, then you can limit your review to that approach, which will save you a lot of time and effort.

ELIGIBILITY CRITERIA

Once you have decided on the broad type of publication you will summarize, the content of the publications needs to be addressed. It is a good idea to think through in advance what should be included in the literature review, rather than waiting to see what turns up in the searches. Trying to summarize a research field without a plan is overwhelming, it cannot be systematic, and you will not be able to easily go back and revise it, let alone replicate or reproduce it.

The review protocol that was introduced in Chapter 1 is a critical tool here. In addition to providing the outline of the review—review question, review methods, review results, and so on—a review protocol formulates eligibility criteria. There are two types of criteria: inclusion (what you want) and exclusion (what you don't want). However, both are, strictly speaking, eligibility criteria because at the time of the review protocol, you do not know yet what exactly you will find (you may have the intention of including certain studies but maybe no studies of that kind have been published yet). At this stage, you are determining what type of material you want to include in your review; only at the end of the review will you know whether the information is available in the research literature.

It's best to use a framework to organize the eligibility criteria. One of the earliest frameworks for literature reviews is PICO. It stands for Patient or Problem (e.g., the clinical condition), Intervention (e.g., the treatment of interest), Comparison (the alternative that the intervention is compared against), and Outcome (e.g., how the effects are measured). Many variations of this framework exist, and in some research areas, several dimensions have been added (e.g., Setting). PICO is most relevant to medical intervention and psychotherapy literature that help answer clinical questions. However, it is always a good idea to use a framework covering key dimensions such as Population, Independent variable or Intervention/Exposure, Measure, and Study design (PI/EMS), which are applicable to most literature reviews:

- Population

    The population criterion encourages you to characterize the study population that is included in the research you are looking for. A very broad characterization is "Are you looking for children or adults or both?"
- Independent variable or intervention/exposure

    The intervention is the independent variable in an experiment (the part you manipulate to find out its effects). It is the treatment the treatment group receives in intervention research studies. In the context of observational studies, this domain is the exposure of interest (e.g., classroom size when you are evaluating the effect of classroom size on school grades). In any other context this is the element that you think will have an effect on something or someone (e.g., personality traits when you are evaluating the effect of personality traits on college success).

- Measure

    This dimension should characterize the type of data you are interested in, that is, what the study should assess and report on to be of interest to you. This is about the type of assessment and the measure (e.g., test scores) that were used to determine whether there was an effect or what kind of effect there was. This is the dependent variable in experiments. In the biomedical literature this is the outcome or effect measure.

- Study design

    This dimension focuses on the type of publication, research study, and methodological approach you are looking for. Are you interested only in empirical studies that report data, or theoretical papers as well? Can the study be a write-up of an experiment or an observational study? Must the publication report quantitative or qualitative data to be of interest? Does the paper need to report a particular analytic method (e.g., multivariate analysis)? And so forth.

As discussed earlier, selecting studies to be reviewed is a critical aspect of your literature review. A framework such as PI/EMS helps to center the review and will be instrumental in defining the review scope. Carefully formulated eligibility criteria will help you locate the best research publications for your literature review.

Of note, restricting searches to a specific study design will help keep the number of publications to review manageable. And, as mentioned in Chapter 3, many databases index study designs, so even before the inclusion screening process has fully started, you can keep the search yield manageable by restricting searches to selected categories. An example is restricting your literature review to publications indexed as experimental studies. However, do consult a librarian to find out how reliable the indexing is for the database you are working with (not all databases are as well maintained as PubMed, and even PubMed indexers can get it wrong sometimes).

In addition to the content criteria, your review may include other limiters, and these should be communicated as eligibility criteria. You may restrict your review to English-language publications; publications within a set period (e.g., published within the past 5 years); publications that are not in an abbreviated format, such as conference abstracts; and/or publications that are readily available as full text. Restricting searches to readily available research takes advantage of the fact that many journal articles are now available free of charge (open access) and are instantly downloadable. It is reasonable to restrict your search to those, especially in smaller projects, but keep in mind that this approach will cause you to miss some relevant papers.

Conceptually, eligibility criteria should be understood as "necessary information a publication needs to report" to be of interest for the review, so the criteria describe the key variables that decide whether a study will be included or excluded from the review. Think through what would be the most informative publications that will help to answer your review question, and then formulate tight inclusion criteria. Describing the inclusion criteria will jog your memory for a later time, help the reader understand the review better, and make the literature selection reproducible and transparent.

INCLUSION SCREENING

Inclusion screening is a central aspect of literature reviews, but it should be understood as a two-stage process: screening at the title and abstract level and at the full-text level. This two-stage process is used because research databases such as PsycINFO are often used for literature searches. These databases generate a list of citations that meet the search criteria and constitute the search yield. These lists include the bibliographic information and some additional pieces, such as the abstract or keywords. But, as explained in Chapter 3, citation records are only a kind of preview, and they include only limited information.

Citation Screening

So, what do you do with the citations that your searches have identified? Research databases include the full citation of the research publication, including the list of authors, the publication year, the title, the journal it was published in, the number of pages, and the publication language. All these pieces of information are useful; for example, the number of pages tells you whether the citation is in an abbreviated form (e.g., a conference abstract), an unusual form (e.g., a letter to the editor), or a more traditional form (e.g., a report of a research study). In addition, many databases also have a record of the abstract, which is a short structured summary of the publication. At the citation screening stage, also called the title and abstract stage, you need to decide whether the publication being cited is likely to be interesting for your review. You know already that not all the citations that came up in the literature search will be relevant for your purposes. As a general rule of thumb, you can expect that only about 10% of citations that the literature search generated will be relevant. For you, the next step is to screen the search yield for relevance.

At this citation screening level, the decision is a judgment call based on limited information. Only at the full-text inclusion screening stage can you apply the explicit eligibility criteria. Titles and abstracts of publications may not be clear or helpful, and many citations that sounded interesting will turn out not to be relevant once you see the full text of the publication. However, the validity threat for the review is that you miss relevant publications during this screen, that is, you overlook citations of publications that are relevant to your review question. Of note, in systematic reviews, this step is done in duplicate, meaning that two independent reviewers do it to ensure that no potentially relevant publication is accidentally missed. For a larger review project, you may be able to team up with another student to have two independent screeners.

Citation Screening Practicalities

So after you have searched a source, what should you do with the search yield, and when should you screen it for relevance? Unless you are reviewing an obscure topic, your search will find lots of material that needs to be screened for relevance. In my experience it is best to import the material into a citation manager rather than try to screen in the original research database. That way you can do the screening in your own time, do not have to worry about Web sessions timing out, can revisit the work (e.g., if you change your mind about an eligibility screening criterion), and can establish a database that is the basis of your own review. Chapter 5 will take you through the process of using a citation manager.

Full-Text Publication Screening

The second inclusion screening stage is the full-text screening stage. This stage happens when you have screened the citations, selected those citations for which you want to see the full-text publication, and have obtained a full-text copy of each article. During the full-text inclusion screening stage, you should then apply your eligibility criteria, that is, a set of inclusion and exclusion criteria. At this stage you have all the information you will ever get (unless you write to the authors), so now you need to decide whether the publication is relevant for your review or not.

The validity of your review rests in part on adhering to these explicit criteria. Doing so ensures that the process of including or not including a publication is transparent and can be communicated through the criteria that function as decision rules. In systematic reviews, this screening process is often also performed in duplicate, and all disagreements between reviewers are resolved through discussion to avoid reviewer errors and bias.

Keep in mind that even if you formulated explicit inclusion and exclusion criteria at your review protocol stage, the criteria may need to be refined further when unforeseen publications turn up and you need to decide whether to include or exclude them in your review (e.g., you find a simulation study when your protocol only addresses empirical data studies).

Publication Screening Practicalities

So, now that you have obtained full-text copies of the papers you want to screen further—what's the next step? Chapter 5 will talk more about

Gio's Gender Differences Review

Gio's thesis addresses gender differences in the response to psychotherapy. He wants to show where his research fits into the existing literature and to provide a brief overview of the existing research studies. He quickly realizes that he needs to find some criteria that he can apply to the thousands of research citations on gender differences that he has identified. He decides to keep publications for his write-up only if they address gender differences in adults (Population; not children, not animals), specifically in the context of psychotherapy (Intervention; psychological treatment of psychological conditions, not all medical issues or therapies), and gender differences in the response to treatment (Measure; not differences in the prevalence of psychological issues) and are reviews or empirical studies (Study design; literature reviews or studies evaluating the effects of an intervention, not opinion papers). He doesn't add the methodology to his thesis because he is already over the recommended word limit for the overall thesis, and the literature review was meant to be only a small part to frame his research. Instead, he puts in the results of the review that adhered to the criteria above. A nice side effect of his approach is that he is confident he found the most relevant literature; because he had a focused area, he was able to digest the findings, which in turn helped him to clarify what his own research will add to the existing research base.

the best format for screening and recording decisions and will take you through the practicalities. This chapter introduces you to the general concept of inclusion screening.

ORGANIZING YOUR MATERIAL

The inclusion screening process described above is borrowed from a systematic review approach, and as usual you need to decide how much, and how strictly, you want to follow the procedure for your own literature review. Whereas some steps, such as categorizing everything, may seem like additional work, the process is designed to help you sort the wealth of material that you have located in your searches into broad buckets. Only a fraction of citations that turn up in the searches will be relevant, and only a fraction of the publications that you have reviewed in detail will be useful for the review (the rule of thumb is also 10% in this stage), so this step consists of screening out irrelevant material and sorting the rest. I personally divide publications into three categories: Include, Exclude, and Background paper/multiple publication/ other. In this system, there are the *Includes*, that is, the material for your literature review, and these publications are different from everything else. These publications are the ones that meet all your inclusion criteria. This is what you will be working with in your literature review; this is what you really wanted to find and about which you want to say more.

Then there are the *Excludes*, that is, papers that are not relevant to your review. The publications may have come up in the initial search but are not what you want. They may have even looked interesting during citation screening, but when you apply your formal eligibility criteria (full-text screening stage), you see that they are not quite right for your review and that you can safely drop them from your radar.

And then there is a third group of other material that is neither in nor out. This lot is more diverse. It consists of *Background* papers that

you may want to cite when framing your review, such as when defining what your review is about. Other reviews that you want to use for
reference-mining will also fall under this category. For example, you may
find a review that you do not want to summarize, but you may use it as a
resource to find primary research studies that you are looking for. Tagging
the publications as "background" will help you keep track of them because
they are neither Includes or Excludes.

Multiple publications also fall in this category. Many studies are
reported in more than one publication. I often see studies now that are
published in a half dozen or more different outlets. There may be a
published protocol outlining the methodology of the study, an entry in
a research registry, a concise journal paper reporting the main results, a
detailed research report published on the university website, a long-term
follow-up paper, a subgroup analysis, another publication focusing on a
different measure or study characteristic, and an editorial talking about
the study. However, all the publications are still reporting on the same
study participants. What is different is the information that is given about
the study. It would be unfair to treat these eight publications as eight
different studies when they all report on the same participants. You will
see that at times the literature review process will feel like detective work
because research authors do not always make it obvious which publications report on the same research study. The different publications will
help to give a complete picture, but the unit of analysis should still be one
study, not eight publications. When you find more than one paper relating
to the same study, you need to decide which publication you declare the
main publication (Include) and which are the accompanying papers (i.e.,
the multiple publications). As a general rule, the main publication should
be the one that is most useful to you and your review, such as the main
publication reporting on the main results. If you have different publications and you can't decide which one is best, use the publication with the
earliest publication year.

Designating some of the material as Includes and separating these
papers (mentally and physically) from other stuff is a helpful approach
to staying organized. It is a good idea to literally sort your material into

different stacks based on the inclusion screening decisions. After this full-text inclusion screening process, you have a set of publications that will be the basis of your literature review.

DOCUMENTING PRESENCE AND ABSENCE OF RESEARCH

Explicit eligibility criteria make it transparent which publications you were looking for and which not, and if you document the criteria, the reader will have a much better understanding of the scope of the review. The eligibility criteria are a way to operationalize the scope of your review—in other words, you are translating the review scope into concrete decision rules for which publications are included in your review and which are not.

A final aspect of explicit eligibility criteria is that your review will be able to document gaps in the literature. It is very easy to communicate the presence of research because the reader will just see what's there and what you are describing in your review. But when publications are absent, the reader will not know why. Eligibility criteria document that you have looked for specific publications, and it will be clear that they do not exist (or, granted, that you didn't find them), not that you did not look for them. Hence you can clearly document the lack of research in an area. For readers of the review this means that they can evaluate the presence and the absence of research and the presence and absence of evidence (i.e., the question cannot be answered despite explicit attempts to find answers).

SELECTING MATERIAL FOR YOUR REVIEW

To produce a manageable review, think about the most informative publications that will help you answer your review question and then formulate tight inclusion criteria. For your purposes, it may be appropriate to simply find the most cited articles on the topic if you are preparing only a brief research introduction (see Chapter 2; see also Chapter 9 for additional ideas for introductions and background sections). In many cases you may have to give examples of research studies rather than try to incorporate everything you have identified in your searches in the text. Using a framework for eligibility criteria will help you think about the identified search yield and select the right examples. The right kind of material in terms of both the level (primary research or secondary literature) and the type of research (the kind of study or scientific publication) will depend on your project as well as your topic.

Just keep in mind that the idea is to find a structured approach to selecting literature. As you can imagine, a review can make almost any point you want it to make because there is always a study out there with unusual results. For your literature review you want to make sure that you are producing a reliable and valid overview. Your review does not need to be comprehensive, but it should not be misleading. Although you probably cannot locate every relevant paper under the sun for your review, you want to be sure that your material selection is not grossly biased or a haphazard selection.

All methods up to this point in the book are designed to help you select material for your literature review; the remaining chapters are about what to do with the material.

CHAPTER 4 ACTION STEPS

☐ Decide (broadly) what types of publications you want to review.
☐ Work out a framework for eligibility criteria (e.g., PI/EMS) to structure what you are looking for in publications.
☐ Formulate inclusion and exclusion criteria to characterize what papers need to report in order to be included in your literature review.

How to Organize:
Managing Your Material

For your literature review, record keeping is critical. This chapter delves into the practicalities of storing the material that will go into your literature review. Whereas the previous chapters were about planning the review and finding and selecting material, this chapter helps you organize it all.

> If you imagine this stage as part of the dinner party we've been planning throughout the book, we are now arranging the ingredients we have bought and what we had at home to get ready to cook.

As you search the literature, you will find thousands of citations, and although they will not all be relevant, you will need to find a way to store

http://dx.doi.org/10.1037/0000155-006
Conducting Your Literature Review, by S. Hempel

what you have found. Search yields and stacks of full-text material can get overwhelming, and you need to find a way to keep track of what you have already looked at. It is also important to have all the Includes in the literature review stored in one place.

It is possible to organize all your material manually, but this chapter shows several ways in which citation management software is useful. If you are absolutely against using citation management software (e.g., you want to use stacks of paper copies and manually type in the details for the literature you are citing), you should go straight to the section called Organizing and Categorizing Your Literature Review Material.

USING CITATION MANAGERS

A *citation management program* (or reference manager) compiles all citations, stores them in a structured way, and organizes them in a database. An electronic citation database has advantages at all stages of the review conduct and write-up.

At the stage of collecting material for the review, a database is useful because it allows you to sort and search the material easily. You will find that some publications come up multiple times in different searches. In addition, many authors have published more than one article on a topic, which makes it very difficult to decide from memory whether you have already reviewed a specific publication or not. Your literature review will also likely involve multiple sources (e.g., PsycINFO and ERIC), and some research will be indexed in both. Storing the results of all literature searches in one central place has the advantage that duplicate publications can be recognized. Citation management programs can automatically discard duplicates from multiple searches so that your database will store only unique citations. Each unique citation in the database will be assigned a unique identifier that you can use throughout your project.

Several commercial (e.g., EndNote) and free (e.g., Mendeley) programs are available. You will want to investigate whether your university has a preference or even provides software for students.

Helpful Resource

Citation managers vary in format and functionality. See Wikipedia for an overview (https://en.wikipedia.org/wiki/Comparison_of_reference_management_software).

Record Keeping for Searches

Using a citation management program also allows you to import results of searches from databases such as PsycINFO while preserving the structure and field content in a machine-readable format. Many programs also enable you to import the information the database has added, such as the abstract or useful keywords to characterize the publication (e.g., indexing terms, as discussed in Chapter 4). Figure 5.1 is a screenshot showing how to download citations from a research database (PubMed) to get them into your own citation management database. You can choose from different download formats. The selected format in this case (MEDLINE) downloads information from all fields. The process is similar for all research databases. If you cannot find a good explanation in the database documentation for how to export searches, ask a librarian—they will definitely know.

At this point you might be thinking, "Why do I need to learn how to export citations? I just want to write my literature review!" The reason is that it is much easier and much faster to import citations into your citation manager than it is to manually add them one by one. A little more work on the front end will help the pieces fall in place quickly and easily when it comes to the actual writing.

Citation management programs are designed to import citations from research databases. Many new programs also allow storing other material such as websites. In addition, some citation managers can also be used to store the full-text material for the literature review. Some programs will allow you to store a PDF of the publication for citations of interest. That way all your literature review material is in one place.

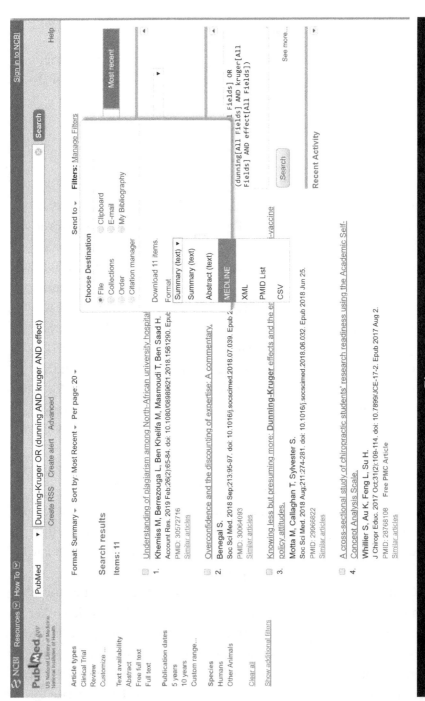

Figure 5.1

Example download from a research database.

Keeping Notes on Citations

Another advantage of having the citations in a database is that you can annotate them. Most citations that come up in a literature search are not relevant and will ultimately not be included in your literature review. A citation management program allows you to add the decisions of the citation screening process. Inclusion screening the titles and abstracts can be best done in reference management software. You download your search yield as described previously. Then once you have all the citations in one place and have discarded duplicates, you can fully concentrate on the relevance of the citations and store your decisions at the same time.

INCLUSION SCREENING IN A CITATION MANAGER

Different citation managers have different setups, so it is worth exploring how best to do inclusion screening. For example, a program may allow you to group citations (e.g., you add a group for all citations that you want to obtain as a full-text publication). Within each grouping the software will let you decide what you want to display. Typically, you will want to display the unique identifier, author, publication year of the publication, title, and your note fields. If you order your database by unique identifier, you can screen your citations in numerical order.

Figure 5.2 shows a screenshot of a citation manager software program that divides the screen neatly for you. You see the unique ID, the titles of the citations, and the abstract. One note field is being used to display the source (where the citation came from). In this view you can easily screen citations by looking at the titles. By using the up and down arrow keys on your computer, you can go from title to title without taking your eyes off the screen. In many cases, you will be able to see from the title of the citation whether it is relevant to your review. In other cases, you will need to read the abstract of the citation. In a screen layout that shows the abstract of your selected citation at the bottom, you can do this effortlessly. To record your decision, you can click on the title that opens the record for this citation and then add your decision to a note field. Remember that at this citation screening stage, you have to

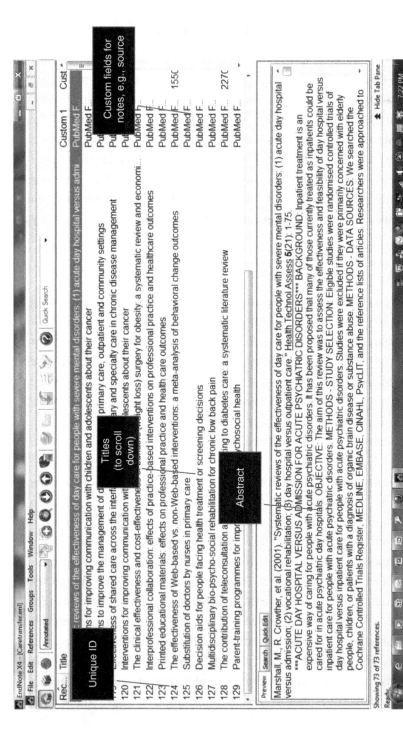

Figure 5.2

Reference management software screenshot. Contains information licensed under the Non-Commercial Government Licence v2.0, United Kingdom. Screen capture from EndNote. ©2019 Clarivate.

decide only whether you want to look at the full-text article or not, so the decision is "order/obtain as full text" or "exclude." The other way to inclusion screen is to create a group (e.g., called "order") and then drag all citations you want to order into that group.

When you have screened your citations and have all the relevant ones in one group, you can annotate them (i.e., add a decision to a note field for all of them). Notes on which citations should be obtained as full text and which ones should be included in the review will help you tremendously with staying organized.

In addition to recording the citation inclusion screening decisions, storing review process information is also very useful. For example, if a citation is not readily available as full text, you can record that in your database. You can track whether and when you requested the full text from your library.

You can also use your citation manager to record the next screening step, that is, full-text screening, which is the final decision. Remember this categorization system:

- Include
- Exclude
- Background paper/Multiple publication/Other

By recording which of the many citations are included, you will have all your included studies (i.e., those that you want to describe in your literature review) in one place and can work with them as a group (the Includes). You can generate a reference list of the Includes for your literature review (a bibliography) or cite them easily in the text of your review report.

Selection Transparency

Using a central database to store your identified citations will also ensure transparency of the review process. It is common practice in systematic reviews to provide an overview of the literature flow, that is, document how many citations were initially identified; how many of these identified

Barbara's Burnout Review

Barbara is helping a researcher to write up a research study on burnout. She has important citations in e-mails, she has some printouts of articles that she wants to reference, someone has started a literature collection for the project, and there are also critical citations in the original research proposal that she doesn't want to forget. She finds out that her university provides students with a specific citation management program. She uses that program to enter all relevant citations into one database so that she has them all in one place. She uses the citation manager for the project report by adding citations to the text and then generating a reference list for the report. After the report is done, the team decides to write up the results of the research as a journal manuscript. Barbara finds the journal's citation style in her citation manager, applies it to her document, and instantly reformats the citations so that the manuscript matches the journal's citation style.

publications were obtained and screened for inclusion as full text; and how many of these full-text publications were included in the review. That way the reader knows how comprehensive the search was and can follow what happened to the identified citations. For systematic reviews, it is essential that all citations are accounted for and the reasons for exclusion of publications are clearly stated. These reviews require that the reason for exclusion is documented at least for all citations that have been obtained as full text (which indicates that the citation looked relevant, at least initially).

Although documenting the results of the inclusion screening process may sound like a lot of additional work, keeping simple notes on why a publication was ultimately not used for the literature review will ensure a systematic approach because it makes the process transparent and ensures that all citations of interest have been followed up on. In a larger project, this process will also save time and effort in the long term because it leaves no room for second-guessing ("Did I forget to include this publication?"), and you will not have to rereview citations or publications that you come across again and that look relevant while trying to remember what the issue was with those particular articles. The best approach to recording why a publication was not relevant is to use the eligibility criteria framework to design a simple system of reasons for exclusion. So, you may have the category "Exclude—Population" because the study sample was not what you were interested in (e.g., you are working on shyness in children, and the publication was about adults). Or, you could have a category for "Exclude—Study design" because the publication did not fall under any of the study design categories that you wanted to summarize (e.g., you are interested in diagnostic accuracy studies, but the publication describes other test characteristics).

Literature Flow

The literature flow for your literature review and the reasons for exclusion can be summarized in a figure called a *literature flow diagram*. Having a literature flow diagram is standard in systematic reviews, scoping reviews, and meta-analyses. Transparently showing the literature flow, from identified citations in searches to the number of studies included in the literature review, or providing reasons for exclusion of publications is particularly useful for readers. Figure 5.3 is an example of a literature flow diagram. Alternatively, you can use the Preferred Reporting Items for Systematic Reviews and Meta-Analyses tool (see the Helpful Resources box at the end of Chapter 9).

Similarly, to allow peer reviewers to determine whether all relevant studies have been considered, you can add a list of excluded citations to the appendix of a review together with the reason for exclusion. That way the reader knows what was screened and for what reason a particular publication was or was not included in the review (assuring the reader that the citation was assessed for eligibility and not just overlooked).

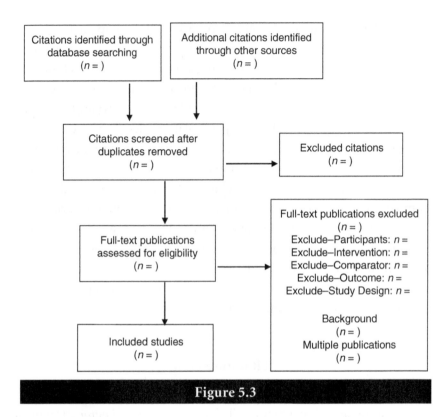

Figure 5.3

Literature flow diagram.

If you are planning to provide a flow diagram or a list of excluded studies with reasons for exclusion, practically that means that the reason for exclusion must be stored together with the citation in a database such as your citation management program. Storing the exclusion reasons (e.g., Exclude—Population, Exclude—Study design) in the citation manager has the advantage that it can be printed out together with the citation. That way you can put together an annotated list of excluded publications. To do this, you add the field with the exclusion decision to the reference style (the help function in the program will show you how to do this), so that the reason for exclusion is noted at the end of each citation in the reference list. Alternatively, you can easily group the citations by reason for exclusion and export separate citation lists for each exclusion category. And in both cases, this does not need to be done manually. Storing the decision information with the citations means that you can instantly generate these lists.

ORGANIZING AND CATEGORIZING YOUR LITERATURE REVIEW MATERIAL

At this point in your review you have selected the material that is the basis of your literature review. The format of the material may vary (e.g., scientific journal papers, books, conference abstracts), and you may have paper copies of some publications and electronic copies of others.

Electronic Records

Because research databases provide access to electronic copies of research articles, you may have some or all of your material in an electronic format. It is a good idea to systematically download and file the PDFs of material that you will include in your literature review. You will be amazed by how often you will need specific papers again if you continue working in a research area. And even with the best memory, it is often helpful to have papers in electronic format so that you can search them electronically.

Some citation managers let you store PDFs in the software, so they are very easy to locate. However, if you need to store the PDFs separately, it is very useful to come up with a system of naming publication files so that you can find them again. Using the name of the first author and the publication year, combined with the unique reference manager ID or parts of the title, will help you find the PDFs again when you need them. An example is "001_Cialdini_2009": This is the first reference in your citation library for your review, Cialdini is the last name of the first author of the publication, and the article was published in 2009. You could also use "001_Cialdini_2009_Breakup" in case you want to store a bit of the title so you can remember the publication more easily. At this point you would add folders to sort the material; for example, you could have one folder for Includes and one for everything else.

Having an accessible electronic copy also lets you share the material easily with coauthors or project collaborators and makes it easier to work with the material. Articles published in open-access journals are instantly accessible as a PDF and downloadable for free, so you can share these publications by providing the web link. Publications with Creative Commons or International Association of Scientific, Technical and Medical Publishers licenses will even allow you to republish limited amounts of information (e.g., a figure) in the body of your own work, as long as you cite the source material appropriately. But always keep in mind that most scientific publications are subject to copyright restrictions. Sharing full text of your literature review material on your website would make for a very transparent review but is not feasible because you would likely be committing copyright infringement.

Helpful Resource

Before sending a full-text PDF you've downloaded to someone else, and certainly before reproducing tables, graphics, or text passages from individual publications in your own work, check the copyright status. More information about open-access publications and Creative Commons licenses can be found at https://en.wikipedia.org/wiki/Open_access and https://creativecommons.org/licenses

Paper-Based Records

It is unlikely that you will have only paper-based material such as a stack of books for your review. But you might have a combination of hard copies and PDFs. If you have paper versions of your material, then it is a good idea to physically sort your material into different stacks. You may want to have a stack for Includes, a stack for Background papers, and a stack for Excludes. Any multiple publications (i.e., more information on an included study) can be either stapled to the included article or otherwise kept together with the Include (note the number of papers if you are accounting for the literature flow). It can also be helpful to staple a form to the first page of each article that clearly shows your inclusion screening decision. Alternatively, you could mark the copy with the decision or use color-coding. You may decide to order your stack of Includes in alphabetical order so that you can find studies easily, or you may order them by the characteristic that you use to structure your write-up (see Chapter 8). When it comes to writing up the results of the review, it is a good idea to keep on your desk only the stack of papers that you want to work with. This will help you focus.

Regardless of whether you use printouts, electronic articles, or a combination, you will want to have a central record of your citations using a citation management system so that you can keep track of your literature review material.

CITING MATERIAL AND CREATING A BIBLIOGRAPHY

Throughout your literature review write-up you will want to cite the material that you have identified. Storing citations in a database means you can export the citations easily into your write-up. Some citation programs are linked to text processing programs; for example, EndNote and Microsoft Word let you cite as you write by linking the citations that are stored in the citation database with the text in your word processing program. This system automatically keeps track of cited literature and can also easily generate the bibliography for you after the review is complete. Keep in mind that each Include should be cited in the text somewhere, so that the complete list of included publications is shown in the bibliography of your literature review. If you are not planning to call out each Include in your write-up (e.g., because you have listed them all in a table and will highlight only some examples in the text), you can start your results section by citing all Includes (that way they definitely will all appear in the reference section).

Even if you insert references manually into your text, a reference manager will be useful because it lets you establish a bibliography for your review in an instant. Once the literature review is complete, it will need a reference list with cited publications. The database will enable you to select the relevant citations you want to cite, and you will be able to copy and paste these references into your review write-up.

Finally, a critical advantage of using a citation management program is the ability to effortlessly adjust the reference style. This guarantees that the bibliography of the review is formatted correctly for the original purpose (e.g., APA Style is standard for a university assignment in the social sciences). It also allows you to reformat the text instantly for other purposes, such as when you want to use the literature review in a journal manuscript. The program will use the journal-specific style and adjust the references accordingly without you having to edit each citation manually.

CHAPTER 5 ACTION STEPS

☐ Find a citation management system that works for you.
☐ Go through a process of screening citations for potential Includes (title and abstract screening).
☐ Identify your Includes (i.e., the material you want to say more about in your review).
☐ Find a way to clearly separate Includes from Excludes (e.g., tag Includes in your citation database; put all Includes in one pile on your desk and label them).
☐ Create a reference list for your literature review (i.e., a list of all the material you are citing in your review).

6

How to Abstract:
Extracting Key Information
From the Literature

This chapter is about data abstraction, the step in your literature review that takes place once you have collected everything that you want to summarize. This step is equivalent to note taking, that is, making notes of what you want to say about the material you have identified.

In keeping with our food metaphor, data abstraction consists of the chopping and preparing steps that take place before any food goes into the pan or oven.

It is, of course, possible to summarize your material without any further structured literature review steps. However, the more complex a topic is and the more publications you are working with, the more important it will be to build a step of data abstraction into your literature review.

http://dx.doi.org/10.1037/0000155-007
Conducting Your Literature Review, by S. Hempel

Data abstraction is the process of extracting key information from the publications that you want to cover in the literature review.

Data abstraction is a way to facilitate a structured overview. It involves coding or charting, summarizing, organizing, and prioritizing the aspects of the material that will be presented in the literature review. It is difficult to describe the astonishing difference between the first impression of skimming the publications you want to summarize and the thorough overview you get after you have systematically abstracted information from your material. Even the most basic data extraction process in which you look for only two or three pieces of information from each publication will help enormously to organize the material that you are working with.

USING A DATA EXTRACTION FORM

To ensure you capture the same specific pieces of information from each full-text document, you will need a data extraction form. You can do this process four different ways. You can work either in the final display format or in an intermediate format (and there are three intermediate format options). All these have advantages and disadvantages. An example of a final display is a table put together in Word processing software that you can copy and paste into your literature review write-up or that you can print to help you write up the review. Chapter 8 has an example (see Table 8.1). The advantage is that it is ready to use. The disadvantage is that extracting your data directly into a table results in a big table, which can be difficult to handle, particularly when it comes to being consistent throughout. Going directly to a table means that you need to set up the format right away—possibly before you know what you want each column to be. As you change column titles and move data around, it can be easy to mess up the format or accidentally delete information.

The second way to do data extraction is in spreadsheet software such as Excel or Google Sheets. Some programs assist you with data entry by providing the option of dropdown menus that you can set up in advance (so instead of typing in free text you can select an answer category from the menu you've set up). Dropdowns are convenient but also important for consistency, so that you are always using the same term for the same category and you avoid spelling mistakes. Spreadsheet programs often also have a word recognition feature whereby the program guesses what you want to say if a category has been used before, and that saves you from having to type out the full word again.

Third, you can use software that has a form or mask setup whereby you enter the information while the data are collected in tabular format. This type is convenient because it lets you add lots of instructions and reminders to the form screen, which will be helpful for consistency at the time as well as later, say, when you find an additional study that should also be abstracted. The data that you enter in the mask are collected in a spreadsheet that can be easily exported, capturing just the data without the instructions. You can use commercial database software (e.g., MS Access) or free software such as Google Forms. You can choose from different variable formats, such as free text or multiple-choice answer mode for categorical answers.

Fourth, there is specific software for literature reviews. Some systematic reviewers, for example, use Covidence for the data extraction. The

Helpful Resources

Google Sheets (free software) is a spreadsheet software that lets you enter data in tabulated format (https://docs.google.com/spreadsheets).

Google Forms (free software) can serve as a data entry form that lets you add instructions to the questions or data collection variables while the answers are collected in a flat database that can be exported as a spreadsheet (https://www.google.com/forms/about/).

Covidence, a program made for literature reviews, can be used for inclusion screening and data abstraction. It is nonprofit software (but it is not free) and can be accessed at https://www.covidence.org.

system supports the literature flow and lets you enter decisions about citations (citation screening), full-text decisions (full-text screening), and then detailed data extraction for publications meeting inclusion criteria. Systematic review software has other advantages; for example, some systems have a machine learning algorithm that learns your inclusion screening decisions from a small sample and then applies them to the rest of your searches. But these software options can be quite pricey.

It is often not necessary for standard literature reviews to use specific data abstraction software, especially if you are not dealing with hundreds of publications and are not planning on preparing data for a statistical meta-analysis. Figure 6.1 shows an example of a short data abstraction form. In this example, a software program is used that captures the responses (what you put on the lines after the variable name). That part can be exported into other programs and used to put a table together, for example. The form, however, includes the variables to abstract as well as instructions for what exactly to extract, in which format, and in how much detail. These instructions are memory aids, and they will help you remember when you write up your literature review what exactly you

---

Study ID: _____
(First author, publication year, unique number from citation manager)

Population: _____
(Five attributes max that characterize this sample)

Method: _____
(Study design [use categories from list, uncontrolled or controlled], analytic method [simple prediction vs. multivariate analysis])

Results:
_____
(Results for the outcome of interest [specify scale], mean & measure of dispersion or numerator and denominator; p value; clarify direction of effects)

Author's conclusion:
_____
(Full-sentence statement, shorten to one sentence, key results plus stated limitation)

Figure 6.1

Data extraction form example.

have captured. These instructions also ensure that you are consistent in your approach, which is particularly important when you spread out your data entry over days or weeks or after some time you notice another study that needs data abstraction.

Regardless of the software, what is important is to treat the publications as sources of data and to establish a database with key aspects of the literature you want to review and summarize. Establishing a database and systematically extracting the key information in the same format for all included publications will enable a structured overview of the literature.

DATA EXTRACTION VARIABLES

A critical step is to determine the variables that you want to abstract from the publications. These variables compose what you need to know about the publication and what you want to say about each publication in your literature review. Consider this step a structured note-taking exercise. Basic data extraction variables are the publication ID, the population characteristics, study design or methods information, a summary of the results, and/or the author's conclusion. You will need to customize the data extraction so that it meets the needs of your literature review.

Extracting the *ID* of the publication is a key way of identifying the publication in your data set. Usually you need only the name of the first author and the year of the publication (only if the same author has published two or more of your Includes will you need more to distinguish them so that the reader can find the publication in the reference section). Where you are summarizing research studies that have been published in more than one publication, list them all together with the main publication. That way you organize the material for yourself and for your reader.

Extracting information about the *population* is common, but you need to decide whether the population is important—for example, because you are looking at different participant samples and suspect that the results of the study could vary depending on the sample. Rather than free text,

Lulu's Limbic System Review

Lulu wants to write a term paper on the limbic system but is still debating how to structure her literature review. She has identified a stack of papers and books on the topic, and they report all sorts of aspects of the limbic system (anatomic description, structure, function, effect of lesions, correlates, and more). She starts out by jotting down some notes on each publication that will help her remember what she wanted the particular paper for, but that quickly gets messy and unreadable (and she notices that she varies in what and how much detail she puts). She also has the impression that she is reading the same studies again and again or maybe recognizing a publication style because some authors have published several articles on the topic. She finally gives in and makes a short table in a word processing document where she records the publication ID (author, publication year), the main topic (e.g., physiological structure), and what the specific subsection could be that she would want the publication for. The subsections structuring her review evolve a bit after she reads more papers, and her system gets a bit more sophisticated as she reads more papers. She decides to go back to the first papers and match them to the new subsections. Lulu is not planning to use the table she generated as a formal evidence table (see Chapter 8); this document is simply for her to help structure the material. Once she has figured out which papers to discuss in which section of her review, she orders her stack of papers accordingly and then writes her term paper.

you may want broad categories here, such as children versus adults. The population information could be combined or replaced with the setting or context of the study. A way to decide which variable to extract from the publication is to think about whether you need to know the population, setting, or context to fully understand the results.

Typically, something about the *method* is also needed. That can be the study design or analytic method. Think about what would make a reader recognize the study type and what would be helpful to know in the context of your review. For consistency, it is best to come up with your own simple categorization system rather than use the original author's terminology or description of the study design and analytic method.

A summary of the *results* is the most complex aspect of data abstraction because each publication typically describes many results. Deciding which results to extract (and ultimately use in your review) is a critical step for your review. Ideally, you want to record results in as structured a way as possible and restrict yourself to measures that can help answer your review question. You might know in advance that some outcome measures are more important than others, so you could track whether the publication says something about these important outcomes. This approach of organizing the review using prespecified measures is critical for an objective overview of the literature. It is very easy to get lost in individual publications because the authors want to get their point across, highlight results that they find interesting, or want to emphasize some results because other results were disappointing (e.g., the study found something unexpected or a lack of association where the author had expected an association).

For the selected outcome measures you would also need to decide how much information is needed to understand the results. For example, when a publication shows that the intervention group was not statistically significantly different from the control group, you may want to add the sample size or any information about the statistical power of the study. If the study shows a difference in a mean scale score between pre- and postmeasurement timepoints, you may need to provide details on the scale (e.g., the range) so that the reader can interpret the results (the change from a score of 3 to 4 is more impressive for a scale that runs from 1 to 5 than for a scale that ranges from 1 to 100).

Many systematic reviews recalculate effects from the data reported in individual studies. This helps to detect errors and prepares the data for meta-analysis, a data aggregation technique that summarizes results across studies. However, calculating effect sizes has another practical outcome: converting data to a common metric. There are different effect size measures. One is the standardized mean difference, which is calculated by converting the study effect into a measure-independent variable (e.g., it does not matter which rating scale was originally used to measure the effect because the effect is expressed on a standardized scale). Converting to standardized mean differences facilitates comparisons across studies because the results are now comparable. In addition, many readers will be familiar with the interpretation of standardized mean differences (e.g., they will recognize a Cohen's d of 0.8 as a large effect). See Further Reading at the end of this book.

Helpful Resource

The Campbell Collaboration maintains an effect size calculator that lets you convert data from individual studies into effect sizes (https://campbellcollaboration.org/effect-size-calculato.html).

Although converting to effect sizes may be outside the time and resources you have for your literature review, whenever you can, try to standardize information to help compare across Includes. For example, individual studies may report counts (e.g., number of participants with a particular result), but the counts are meaningful only when you know the denominator. For your literature review you should consider converting descriptive data to a proportion so that you can compare easily across studies. So, if studies report the numerator (e.g., 16 participants reported an anxiety attack) and the denominator (e.g., the total number of participants was $N = 58$), to standardize data across studies you would convert these two numbers into a rate or percentage of participants in the sample (e.g., 28% of participants reported an anxiety attack). That saves the reader of your review having to mentally calculate what proportion was affected in each study. Other ways of standardizing are to always use the same format, such as recording data as "mean (SD)" when reporting the mean and standard deviation. Other standardization decisions include keeping the order of reporting consistent (e.g., report variables in the same order), making the number of reported decimal points consistent when abstracting, and deciding whether to leave out the first zero when reporting correlation coefficients or p values and then following through consistently.

Finally, the author's *conclusion* is also a good way to provide an overview. Often it is interesting to see how authors interpret the results and the implications of their opinion. Any data you capture from this portion of a study should be targeted toward the review question you want to answer, so in many cases you will want to extract only a fraction of the overall conclusions.

EXTRACTING AND ABSTRACTING

Data extraction is a combination of taking information directly from the publications you want to summarize and abstracting that information. Abstracting can involve categorizing, quantifying, or other methods of coding or charting the information so that you are able to compare studies and evaluate the reported information.

In many cases, it will be more useful to categorize the information than to copy the exact words or details reported in the publications. Think of this process as a further way to organize your material. At this stage, it is critical to think through what you would likely say about the publication in your review and to work with categories that you think are useful and can be applied in a standardized way across studies.

Another way to organize the review is to try to quantify the information you find. Some aspects of the publications may not fall into distinct categories but can be rated on a continuum that will help describe publications and to differentiate between them. For example, you may want to track the size of studies so in your overview you can order Includes by study size to ensure that large landmark studies are reported first.

As with all aspects of the review, remember to store the instructions, definitions, and description of each category or rating and any decision rules together with the data so that you can easily repeat the steps if you want to add studies to your pool of publications or describe your procedure to the reader in your review.

For some aspects of the publications you may want to be specific and stick as closely to the description in the Include as possible. However, when you are citing the studies using an exact phrase or a full sentence taken from the original publication, you will need to properly quote the study according to APA Style standards. Obviously, keep in mind that copying and pasting from the original publications makes plagiarism all too easy. Think carefully about how much of the original wording is really needed and how it could be paraphrased or reorganized for your review to avoid plagiarism issues (see Chapter 8 of the *Publication Manual of the American Psychological Association, 7th ed.,* for tips on this). Even when you are copying and pasting from the original publications, organize/rearrange the information the same way for all Includes. Consistent reporting will help you with your synthesis of the material and help the reader understand the presented information.

EXPORTING DATA

When selecting a software program to help you with data abstraction, you need to consider ease of input and export of data. As discussed at the beginning of the chapter, some software is specifically designed to facilitate data entry. But knowing how to export the data so that you can use the information easily in your review may be even more critical. You will have no problem when extracting data into a word processing document. It will not offer all the advantages of more specialized software, but the process of standardized data abstraction is the same (extracting the same information for all studies).

Spreadsheet software will help you organize the material you have and often also allow you to perform simple data manipulation tasks such as ordering publications by a variable of your choice (e.g., in alphabetical order or by study size if you have tracked that). Regardless of the order in which you extracted the data initially, you will be able to reorder the Includes according to the variable you decide on, making your write-up easier. Another important function of having the data extraction in spreadsheet format is the ease of selecting specific Includes. For example, you can select Includes that have a specific feature (e.g., select only studies that were conducted in a school setting among all studies and settings in your data set).

MEANS, NOT AN END

Finally, despite the usefulness of structured data abstraction for the literature review, keep in mind that data abstraction is a means, not an end. The data abstraction must be planned and executed with the literature review specification and level of effort in mind. You will likely want to print out the data you have extracted and work through the review write-up with that printout. Or you may want the information to populate an evidence table, a key tool for literature reviews that is described in detail in Chapter 8. But the database with abstracted data is ultimately a storage place for information that aims to facilitate displaying information for the literature review. Only in very rare cases will you share the database with the reader, so it is best to understand it as a temporary product that will help with the final product, that is, your literature review report.

In summary, data abstraction describes the process of selecting information that you want to use from the individual studies. The next two chapters describe how to evaluate the individual Includes further and how to best present the results of your literature evaluation.

CHAPTER 6 ACTION STEPS

☐ Work out what you want to abstract from the Includes (included studies/publications).
☐ Find a suitable format for data abstraction (table, spreadsheet, form, literature review software).
☐ Abstract the information for each Include.

How to Assess: Critically Appraising Your Material

All of the literature review material you are now working with has passed the eligibility criteria. However, just because all publications are relevant does not mean that you must treat them all the same. This chapter looks at critical appraisal, a concept and process you should consider for your literature review.

> If you were preparing a dinner, this would be the stage where you group the ingredients for the individual dishes so that everything goes in the right pot.

A *critical appraisal* process assesses each of the Includes, that is, each study or publication that you want to include in your review. This appraisal means critically reviewing the material you are working with. If you have a broad range of included material, this assessment can be very basic, such as whether the information is based on an opinion or on an empirical study. However, even within narrower categories of publications or study designs (e.g., only clinical trials), studies can vary and do not all need to be treated the same way. The research articles that you have identified will differ in quality, and some of the research will be more important than others for answering your review question. There are numerous ways to assess publications and to differentiate between them. However, in all cases, the concept of critical appraisal—that is, critically reviewing the information you have located—is valuable. For a term paper that summarizes empirical research or a literature review that is part of your thesis, you may want to review the internal and external validity criteria sections. As a minimum, you want to think about where the information is coming from and how trust-worthy it is.

 Nadeem's Neuroticism Review

Nadeem primarily wants his literature review to introduce the concept, definition, and change of use of the psychological trait term *neuroticism*. He does not restrict his review to empirical studies because the research likely started with conceptual consideration and empirical studies would have been tested only in later work. He uses formal and informal sources to find his material. He searches PsycINFO (which looks for his search terms in titles, abstracts, and keywords of citations), but he also makes use of PsycARTICLES because the database lets him search the full text of thousands of psychological articles. He looks up the

Nadeem's Neuroticism Review (*Continued*)

term in Wikipedia and searches for "history of neuroticism"
in his favorite Internet search engine and Google Scholar
(to find the most relevant publications, he uses the Advanced
Search option so that he can find only articles that use the
exact term or that have *neuroticism* and *history* in the title).
He uses these sources as a portal to information, which means
he follows up with the literature that is being cited. Not surpris-
ingly, Nadeem learns the most from existing literature reviews.
He starts writing up what he comes across, but he notices that
he can't keep track of all the nuances, and he keeps forgetting
which aspects were mentioned in which paper as soon as he
looks at more than one issue. Instead, he starts putting a data
extraction table together in which he checks off whether an
article provides information on the history, discusses conceptualization or operationalization (e.g., measurement scales),
and/or includes a formal definition of neuroticism. He doesn't
formally assess his sources of information, but in the write-up
he makes sure to put more emphasis on thorough overviews by
known authors than on papers that make only a specific point.
To help with this task, he sorts the publications into key papers
and other papers. He writes down the criteria that helps him
sort the papers; for example, he notes what characterizes a
thorough overview (e.g., comprehensive, addressing multiple
aspects of interest, perhaps reporting a search and sources, and
having a large number of references) and what he means by
known authors (e.g., authors who published three or more
articles that address neuroticism).

INTERNAL VALIDITY

The *internal validity* of a research study refers to its methodological quality and scientific soundness. One important consideration is the basic study design of the research and the inherent limitations that come with each study design. Strong study designs allow strong evidence statements for empirical studies, whereas weaker study designs are unlikely to lead to definitive answers because it is not possible to rule out confounding or alternative explanations for the observed effects. If you are not familiar with the research area you are reviewing, you may not know the sticky points that can threaten the validity of the studies. For this reason it is a good idea to read existing reviews to see which aspects they emphasize (or ask a content expert, as recommended in Chapter 2).

RISK OF BIAS

Within each study design category are typically several features that have been proposed to differentiate the methodological soundness of studies. For a literature review on a tight timeline and with limited resources, it is best to concentrate on the *risk of bias*. This concept refers to whether the results of the study are likely to be distorted because of the methodological conduct or reporting of the study. Critical appraisal dimensions that people consider in literature reviews of primary research include the following:

- selection bias,
- performance bias,
- detection bias,
- attrition bias, and
- reporting bias.

The main potential for *selection bias* is when you are comparing two groups to assess the effect of an intervention or another variable. The problem is that there may be other differences between the groups that have nothing to do with the intervention or variable of interest and that are then falsely interpreted as effects of the intervention. The random assignment by the study investigator to intervention groups that is common in medical research studies aims to protect from selection bias.

Performance bias assesses whether there may be effects that originate in the knowledge of the study condition (e.g., Hawthorne effect in participants, whereby people behave differently because they know they are under observation). Blinding participants and study personnel so that they do not know what is being studied is a protection against performance bias. For example, the use of a placebo identical in appearance to an experimental drug can create a triple-blind experimental condition (neither patient, nor health care provider, nor study personnel interacting with the patients know whether they are dealing with a placebo or not, and the drug content is known only to an outside entity); this is a standard way to avoid performance bias in medical research. In other research areas, the best protection is using study personnel who do not know the full research hypothesis and participants who do not know what the investigator is testing. However, the latter is not always compatible with informed consent requirements in research studies.

Blinding also serves a key role in avoiding *detection bias*. Using independent outcome assessors—that is, study personnel who take the measurements do not know about the experimental assignments or observation group—is a key protection. All studies with self-report data need to evaluate whether results could be distorted by social desirability or other effects. The participants will know which study condition they were in, so they will not be blind to the research condition, and that knowledge can affect their answers to questionnaires or in interviews.

Attrition bias assesses whether the reported effects of the study are in part a function of study withdrawals; for example, participants who do not like tasks in an experiment may drop out of the study, and the research study would be left with a sample that compares only participants who completed the experimental task and those who are in the control group. In that case a highly selected sample would be compared with a control group, which is problematic, as you can imagine.

Reporting bias describes the purposeful selection of particular results by the study authors, even though more data are available. A basic example is a study in which multiple alternative outcome measures were used but only a measure that showed the effect the author wanted to show was reported. As you know, there are often many ways of analyzing data in a research study, and the solution presented in the research paper may have been chosen because it demonstrated a specific effect. In addition, it is common to report the source of funding (if there was one) together with the study. That helps the reader to decide whether authors are likely to have a conflict of interest and are more motivated to highlight some results than others. Reporting bias is difficult to assess, but it is a good idea to take the credibility of the source of information into account.

EXTERNAL VALIDITY

The *external validity* of a research study refers to the applicability or generalizability of the results. An experiment may be beautifully carried out, internally logical and producing reliable results, but its results may be only partially applicable to your review question. This may be, for example, because it was carried out in a research lab and the context is very different from the real-life conditions and behaviors that you wanted to address in your review. For example, how children learn in a research lab and how they learn in a classroom might be very different. The research study may have used a sample that is not representative of the population you had in mind. Or perhaps the study is assessing an outcome measure that is not central to the review question.

For your review, you may want to rate the relevance of the publication to answer the review question. Again, although you do data abstraction only for publications that have met all eligibility criteria, some Includes may still be more important or more relevant than others and you would want to capture that.

QUALITY OF THE RESEARCH VERSUS QUALITY OF THE REPORTING

For all literature reviews, you need to acknowledge that you are making judgments on the research study based on the information that was reported in the journal publication. Only in rare cases will you be able to go back to original authors for clarification, so you often need to make an educated guess based on what was reported.

When you are assessing research studies, keep in mind that reporting requirements have changed over time. In part, this is a function of reporting guidelines—that is, established guidelines that have been adopted by scientific journals and that require authors to report on critical aspects of the research. Today's research articles are often more detailed than older publications, or at least they are more detailed for methodological aspects that are now considered important. Reviewing reporting guidelines regarding what should have been reported and in how much detail can be helpful for the critical appraisal process.

Helpful Resource

The network EQUATOR (Enhancing the QUAlity and Transparency Of health Research) is a collection of useful tools and has a wide collection of reporting guidelines (http://www.equator-network.org).

The American Psychological Association has also published guidance relevant to psychological research (https://www.apastyle.org/jars).

CRITICAL APPRAISAL SCORING ACROSS DIMENSIONS

The information from the individual dimensions can be combined in different ways. You can use your list of dimensions as a checklist and report how many studies met the criteria that you set forth. You can summarize the results of each dimension into a summary score. The summary score does not need to be a simple addition of each dimension. You could decide that some criteria are more important than others and focus on these. And sometimes you need to know what you want to say about the Include before you can know which critical appraisal dimension result you should point out.

Critical Appraisal Dimensions to Assess

Resource collections can help with critical appraisal in literature reviews, including "living" handbooks, that is, collections that continuously get updated to capture the latest research on evidence synthesis. The *Cochrane Handbook for Systematic Reviews of Interventions* is one of the largest collections of resources and applicable to a broad scope of interventions in the biomedical literature. It has one chapter dedicated to assessing risk of bias in studies that you want to include in a literature review. Note, however, that the handbook addresses only intervention research, not other study designs or other types of research publications.

> **Helpful Resource**
>
> The *Cochrane Handbook for Systematic Reviews of Interventions* is a living handbook that gets continuously updated (http://handbook-5-1.cochrane.org). It contains information on critical appraisal as well as examples of figures and tables to document critical appraisal.

Thousands of checklists for critical appraisal have been published. Published reviews can help you find tools or dimensions that are important to assess in your research area. However, you have to limit your critical appraisal to key dimensions. Assessing publications in a thoughtful, reliable, and valid way is time consuming, so you have to be selective.

Your small set of dimensions to assess can be study design aspects such as the size of the study, analytic aspects such as the lack of controlling for confounding variables, common sources of risk of bias (e.g., selection bias), or external validity aspects (e.g., a study sample may be highly selective and not representative of the population your review aimed to cover). I would suggest limiting the assessment to a handful of dimensions even if your literature review is a larger project. Anything more will be difficult to integrate because there is so much information to consider. If your literature review is only one part of a research study, you need to be even more mindful of resources and the time you can dedicate to this process, and in that case capturing fewer dimensions from each study will allow you to use your time more efficiently. When you are working on a short introduction section, you are unlikely to have a formal procedure for assessing internal and external validity, but you may want to keep the basic principle in mind that not all publications are of the same quality. Even a shorthand process for critically reviewing your literature is better than neglecting the validity of the research altogether.

Critical Appraisal Documentation and Use

You can record your appraisal dimensions and ratings in a table, put them in a figure, add them to the evidence table (see Chapter 8), report them in the text when you describe your Includes, or just apply the criteria (dedicating more space to the best material in the write-up). No matter which dimensions you choose to assess the studies in your review, make sure that you are using the information. Critical appraisal, just like data extraction, is a means, not an end, so it is important to stick to dimensions that you are going to use in your review. More important than laboriously and mechanically rating each study is that you find key dimensions that you think are critical for your review (and there might be only one or two that are essential). That way you can identify and highlight those publications in your review that are best suited to answer the review question.

CHAPTER 7 ACTION STEPS

☐ Work out what you want to assess for each included study/publication (using no more than a handful of criteria).
☐ Assess each Include, applying the same criteria.

8

How to Synthesize: Determining What to Say About the Literature

At this point in the review you have searched and identified the relevant material, you have abstracted and assessed it, and now you are ready to combine the information and summarize the results. This *synthesis* is your unique contribution. This chapter provides a hands-on approach to synthesizing literature.

> Now we are finally cooking: frying and sautéing and boiling and blanching away!

One way of thinking about the synthesis is to envision three parts: a summary of the search results, a summary overview of the Includes, and a summary of the results across Includes. Keep in mind that for your literature review write-up, depending on the type of

http://dx.doi.org/10.1037/0000155-009
Conducting Your Literature Review, by S. Hempel

literature you are working on, you may present only the third part (the summary of findings) in the main text. You should be able to reproduce part one (summary of the search) and should have documentation of part two (summary of individual Includes), but depending on the review specification, the information may go in the appendix of your write-up or remain with you as your review notes. The following shows how you can approach each part of the synthesis.

SUMMARY OF THE SEARCH

After you have completed the review, you should be able to summarize the literature flow. You should be able to say how many citations your searches identified, how many publications you screened as full text, and how many studies met all your eligibility criteria. The last part, the number of included studies, is the unit of analysis in your review. This chapter refers to the included publications as studies, but these do not need to be empirical research studies. Depending on your review, you may have included published theories or other types of publications. But as discussed in Chapter 4, studies may have been published in more than one publication. And the synthesis is about studies, the key unit of analysis, not publications as such, acknowledging that often multiple publications report information on a study.

CHARACTERISTICS OF THE INCLUDES

The second part provides the reader with a short summary of the type of included studies. These may be research studies (potentially published in more than one publication) or other material (e.g., theoretical papers) depending on your review, but these are the study units you are including in your review. You could use the eligibility criteria as a framework and describe what you found for each dimension. For example, you would state the number of studies in what *populations* or *settings*, what kind of *interventions* or exposures they looked at, how many studies reported on which *measure* of interest, and what kind of *study designs* the included studies employed. One thing you should avoid in your literature review is describing each Include in turn. That makes for tedious reading and will not be helpful.

The reader will get a great overview if you can refer to an evidence table. Evidence tables describe each study, with one row per study. The study description is standardized because the table displays the same information for each study. The evidence table should have a place for all central inclusion criteria. Although in the text you give only a broad overview, you can refer the reader to the table for more detail and that way do not need to describe each study at length in the text.

Table 8.1 is an example of a very detailed evidence table to show where various kinds of information could go. Note that the first row in this example provides instructions for what kind of information could go in each cell. The second row shows a fictive example. Evidence tables should be organized by study, with each study being reported in one row. Note that the variables and column structure are always unique to your review. Furthermore, the example includes several categorical designations, such as the study design. The table shows just the labels, so you should provide information on how these labels are defined somewhere in your review write-up (or add it to the notes section of the table).

You should also summarize the results of your critical appraisal of the Includes in this section if you have assessed them. Again, this can be a broad-stroke characterization because you could either add the critical appraisal results to the evidence table or add a separate table; you do not need to describe each score for each criterion. Use examples for points you want to highlight, but overall this section should be short. Again, avoid describing each Include in turn. Instead, move to the next step.

SUMMARY OF THE RESULTS ACROSS INCLUDES

The trick to writing a good literature review is to resist describing one Include after another in one endless list. The reader can see each individual study (or other kind of publication that is relevant to your

Table 8.1

Example Evidence Table With Instructions

ID	Population Setting N	Design Analysis Assessment method Procedure	Analyzed variables	Outcomes Results for the outcome of interest	Authors' conclusion
Author, year (e.g., last name of the first author of the paper and the publication year, i.e., sufficient info for your reader to find the study in your list of references)	Sample characteristics Setting info Number of participants (potentially with information about how many were asked and did not participate)	Study design (use a prespecified list of study designs that are defined in your review write-up) Key analysis feature (use simple categorization scheme if possible) Assessment method (be as concise as possible) Procedural information needed to understand the study (what did they do)	State what exactly was assessed	Analyzed outcomes Focused results documentation	Summary of the conclusion (use abstract, shorten further, and use only relevant statements related to the review)
Pierce, 2002	1st-year psychology students, alumni letter records University of Southern California 100 students	Survey study Multivariate analysis Self-report questionnaires, university records Students filled out a questionnaire about psychologist, student records were linked	Attitudes toward rural settings	Size of city according to the city the alumni newsletter is sent to Negative correlation between attitudes toward rural settings and study size [r -.22]	The data document an association between unfavorable attitudes toward rural settings and place of residence.

review) if you are providing an evidence table, which will provide details on Includes and allow a concise overview. Addressing one Include after another is not a literature *synthesis* and not a good way to summarize research results for the reader. Instead, in this third and most important part of your review, think about ways to summarize across the literature review material. What can you say about the stacks of material you have collected?

For this part of the review, you first need to go back to your review question. Review questions are a critical aspect of the literature review (and you would be surprised to know how often review authors forget to get back to the original question they wanted to answer). It is very easy to get lost in the description of the included studies. But a key characteristic of good literature reviews is that they come back to the big-picture questions and try to answer them.

Furthermore, summarizing findings across your identified material requires an additional tool. You need organizing features that you can use to summarize across included studies. One feature can be the outcome measure—think about what was measured and assessed in the studies. Most helpful here is thinking about constructs (e.g., quality of life, depression symptoms, sleep quality) rather than different instruments used to measure the construct (unless you think this is important for the findings). Describing research findings across studies ordered by the outcome is a key way to combine information in a review of empirical evidence. With this approach, you are keeping one of the variables constant (e.g., the measure), and this will automatically help you to organize the material. You will likely find that reorganizing your material this way will give you a fresh perspective and help you summarize your literature review results.

A summary of findings table is a good way to structure and document the synthesis across studies. Summary of findings tables can be organized by review question, then intervention or exposure or independent variable, and finally outcome measure (the dependent variable, the effect of interest). Most important, different from the evidence table, the summary of findings table is not organized by study. The summary of findings table

Victor's Vocational Test Review

Victor's vocational test literature search found a few studies that report on the validity of career choice tests, and now he has to think through how to best present the results of his review. He wants to answer the question "What is the validity of career choice tests?" He decides to order the synthesis by validity criterion (e.g., construct validity, concurrent validity using similar tests, predictive validity), given that the answer to the question differs according to the kind of validity evidence he is talking about. First, he describes the results of the studies reporting on construct validity, then the studies investigating other types of validity, and finally the few studies reporting on predictive validity. He had hoped the studies could be grouped by prediction measure (e.g., length of stay in selected job) to help him compare and contrast the study results, but the studies each used unique approaches. Instead, he describes the volume of studies for each validity area and documents whether studies found affirmative results (evidence of validity) or not and reports what exactly the positive and the negative studies looked at.

aims to summarize across studies (see Table 8.2). Structuring by features such as outcome measures will help you to synthesize across studies. The table organization forces you to determine how many studies have addressed a particular measure and what the results were.

A further critical way to summarize across publications is to compare and contrast. For empirical research studies, you would summarize findings by comparing and contrasting results across studies, going through each outcome of interest in turn. You thereby document for the reader where research findings agree and where they disagree. In your synthesis try to

Table 8.2

Summary of Findings Table Structure

Review question Intervention/exposure Outcome	Number and types of studies (Number of participants) Reference	Findings	Body of evidence quality
Outcome measure 1			
Outcome measure 2			

determine the recurrent themes or patterns that can be identified across publications and document areas where there is conflicting evidence that the reader should know about, such as where research studies do not agree.

One of the methods in systematic reviews that helps with summarizing empirical research studies is meta-analysis because it provides a numerical summary of findings across studies. Meta-analysis aggregates data across studies, which increases the statistical power compared with individual studies. It can detect small effects that individual studies could not show.

Helpful Resource

Several R packages are available for meta-analysis, including metafor. R is a free software environment, and metafor can be accessed at https://cran.r-project.org/web/packages/metafor/index.html

However, most literature reviews do not use meta-analysis and have no way to increase the statistical power above that of the individual studies. You need to work out a way to decide what the results are and whether evidence across studies is conflicting or not. The method to count positive and negative studies, sometimes called vote counting, is seemingly straightforward but in reality is not that easy and can be very misleading.

For example, when you are evaluating the effect of an intervention or the effect of certain exposure variables, you need to decide what you count as positive or negative. Studies may report the size of the effect and/or the statistical significance of the effect. One critical aspect to consider is the statistical power of individual studies. If a study reports a statistically significant effect, there is no problem. If the study does not find a statistically significant effect and reports a statistical power analysis that shows it had sufficient power, there is also no problem. However, most studies do not report a power analysis, and if they do not find a statistically significant effect, it is hard to know whether the sample was too small to detect an effect or whether there really was no effect. Make sure that you communicate this uncertainty to the reader of your review and when in doubt, report the effect and the confidence interval. For more information on statistical power, see the recommendation in Further Reading.

Finding Your Lens

Note that organizing by outcome measure is not the only approach to reviewing a body of literature, and it may not be appropriate for your review. Not all literature reviews summarize empirical studies that report outcomes. For example, you may have set out to review theoretical perspectives or may be interested in themes identified in qualitative studies. However, the principle is the same: Rather than describing each study or publication (the unit of analysis in your review) in turn, find characteristics that organize the material. Use the variables to structure your synthesis and compare and contrast findings across Includes. For example, if you are reviewing behavior change models, you could structure your review by the complexity of the models, individual included components, or supporting evidence for the models. This is the framework or lens through which you look at the literature review material. This is your unique contribution and it can be a novel and unique way of looking at the literature.

Also keep in mind for the synthesis that even though you have identified all included studies as relevant and contributing to your review, you do not need to treat them all the same. You may have discovered flaws in the research reported in some publications during the critical appraisal process. In this case it is perfectly legitimate to concentrate on some studies more than others in your results section. Some included material will likely be more helpful than others in answering your review questions.

Quality of the Body of Evidence

Keep in mind that in this last step, synthesizing findings across Includes, you are drawing conclusions from a body of evidence. You are using this body of research that you have identified in your literature review to answer your review questions. Whereas all previous steps concentrated on individual studies or publications, at this stage of your review you are bringing the information together and need to synthesize all included material.

In systematic reviews, it is common practice now to differentiate the summary results from an evaluation of the *confidence* in the findings. You may have come to a specific conclusion about the literature. For the reader, it will also be important to know how confident you are in your conclusion. To assess and convey your confidence, you evaluate the quality of evidence you have found. Whereas Chapter 7 was about assessing individual studies, now you are working with the entire body of evidence you have located through your literature review. You are going beyond individual studies and evaluate the group of Includes.

In systematic reviews, the body of evidence evaluation is relatively straightforward for clinical intervention studies. There are rules about how to evaluate a body of evidence and grade evidence statements, that is, use categories to communicate how confident the systematic reviewer is in individual results of the review. The GRADE group has established tools and resources for systematic reviewers. For other literature reviews and other topics it is not as straightforward, but thinking about the body of literature and your confidence in answering your review question is a step that can be useful for many literature reviews.

When you are answering your review questions, you will have a clear answer for some. For other questions, you may have found no relevant literature. Or perhaps you found research that does not allow you to draw sound conclusions because of limitations in the methodology (e.g., there

Helpful Resource

The GRADE (Grading of Recommendations Assessment, Development and Evaluation) Working Group's tool for grading the quality of evidence and the strength of recommendations can be found at http://www.gradeworkinggroup.org

are only pilot studies with preliminary results). Or there may be issues with the findings because the identified Includes reported conflicting results. Or your review may have mainly found that it is complicated because the results may depend on which subgroups or specific settings you are reviewing and there is no obvious pattern. For those review questions, you would need to state that the question cannot be answered or that there are serious caveats associated with your answer. Explain the reason, which may be because there is insufficient literature or because you have serious concerns about whether the identified studies' results correctly represent the answer to the review question.

When you decide how confident you are in your answer to the review question, there are some dimensions that you should think about. A basic question is, of course, the presence of Includes, that is, whether you found studies that answer your review question. Study limitations as outlined in the previous paragraph are another key dimension. Yet another key concept is that of replication. You can ultimately be much more confident in results that have been found by more than one researcher group. Replication by an independent group in a different sample of participants reporting consistent results is critical for confidence in the results. Another way to think about confidence in the answer to the review question is to think about an additional study being published tomorrow. What are the chances that this study would overturn the results of your review? As a very general rule you can assume that the more high-quality studies you have in a body of literature that are showing consistent findings, the more confident you can be.

Ida's Illusionary Superiority Review

Ida is interested in cognitive biases, particularly whether people are more likely to overestimate their own qualities in particular situations (e.g., whether there are conditions or areas where people are more prone to the effect). She looked at a variety of sources and found interesting studies. She abstracted a few details for each study in an evidence table. Then she started a summary of findings table where she noted how many and which studies addressed which cognitive bias (e.g., Dunning–Kruger effect), under which conditions, and what the results were across studies for the bias in the individual conditions. Ida notices that many areas have been studied in only a single research study. She documents the findings for the areas but also makes a note in a quality of evidence column that these results have to be regarded with caution because they have not been replicated yet. They may be outliers or study artifacts, so her confidence in the findings is not high because a future study may either confirm or challenge them. She also has some areas with multiple studies where studies come to different conclusions. In the end she goes with the type of study to determine if there is an effect. If the effect is reported in more than one large study without obvious flaws, she uses those as the basis of the summary. Ida is less concerned about small studies and dissertations not yet published in a scientific journal that seemingly contradict the large studies, but she notes the inconsistencies in her evaluation of the quality of evidence.

CHAPTER 8 ACTION STEPS

- ☐ Avoid describing each Include one after another.
- ☐ Consider using an evidence table to provide an overview of your material.
- ☐ Think about a framework to present the findings of your review, with or without the help of a summary of findings table.
- ☐ Consider the body of literature and communicate your confidence in answering the review question.

How to Document: Writing Up Your Literature Review

Almost there! If you have followed the steps described in this book, your literature review is done—you just need to write it up. This last chapter describes ways to document a literature review. This chapter is all about the write-up, that is, the report, manuscript, chapter, or thesis that you are producing and suggested tables and figures you could use to summarize literature review information.

> After all the cooking, now we are arranging the food nicely on the plate and are setting the table so that we and our guests can enjoy it.

http://dx.doi.org/10.1037/0000155-010
Conducting Your Literature Review, by S. Hempel

USE YOUR STYLE GUIDE
AND FIND GOOD MODELS

Because a literature review involves working with other people's publications, you need to be up to speed on how to best do that. For social sciences and many related research areas, the most recent edition of the *Publication Manual of the American Psychological Association* will be your go-to manual for writing guidance. It shows you how to properly cite articles in your write-up, how to format figures and tables, and how to apply consistent numbering and punctuation styles, among other things. Chapter 6 has already given some tips on how to avoid plagiarism during data abstraction. Chapter 5 introduced you to copyright, which is critical to understand when you want to use published figures or tables for your literature review.

When it comes to applying style rules and all the other principles discussed in this book, it will be really helpful for you to look at examples of published literature reviews. Every article in a scientific journal has a background section, so in your own literature review material you will have dozens of examples. However, keep in mind that authors do not necessarily put this section together systematically. Also, some journals have strict word limits, and authors try to shave off words where they can. If you are working on your thesis, look at examples that others in your department have recently completed. You may find lots of examples that you like in terms of structure and style. Just make sure you look at several examples so that you see different approaches to the literature review section. If you are working on a stand-alone literature review, you will have come across other reviews when you explored your topic (see Chapter 1). You have probably come across examples that you can use as inspiration for your write-up. Also, note that some journals such as the American Psychological Association's (APA's) *Psychological Bulletin* are dedicated to publishing literature reviews. Although these reviews often will be far more complex than your own literature review, you can still look at the approach the authors have taken. You can see how they have structured their write-up and in how much detail they presented the methods. You will also find inspiration regarding the hardest part of

Helpful Resources

The *Publication Manual of the American Psychological Association, Seventh Edition*, which is used for the social and behavioral sciences, can be ordered at https://www.apastyle.org/manual.

  Psychological Bulletin is an example of a journal dedicated to literature reviews (https://www.apa.org/pubs/journals/bul).

the review, which is synthesizing the findings across individual studies (see Chapter 8 for tips).

How you write up your own literature review depends largely on the type of review you are producing. Figure 9.1 populates the visualization you saw in Chapter 1. It gives you an idea of what kind of information you will need to include for each type of review. The remainder of the chapter describes each section in detail.

If you are writing only a background section, be highly selective in what you present. Even if you have followed rigorous and elaborate methods, you need to concentrate your write-up on what you found and also be very selective in what and how much literature you cite. If your literature review is a smaller part of a bigger research project, you may need to work with a compromise, that is, reporting the results of the review in the main text and providing methodological detail in an appendix. Another possibility is to have two documents: one a detailed review protocol that outlines all methods and procedures and the second document dedicated to the results of the review. Only if you are working on a stand-alone literature review project will you likely have enough space to provide more information on the topic, your methods, and the findings of your review.

The following sections compose an outline for a literature review as a stand-alone product. The outline is structured in the same way as a research article write-up. As I've done throughout the book, I present the outline to give you ideas for your write-up; again, how many ideas and which ones you take away depend on your goal, the purpose of the

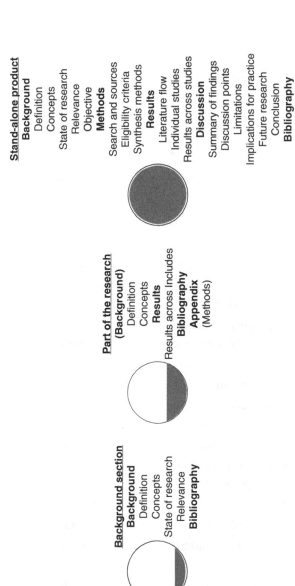

Figure 9.1

Types of review and reporting elements.

review, and your audience. Note that a write-up does not just mean text. Consider using at least one figure (e.g., flow diagram) and at least one table (e.g., evidence table) in your write-up.

BACKGROUND SECTION OF YOUR LITERATURE REVIEW

For a stand-alone literature review write-up, the reader will expect a short background section introducing the research field and an introduction of the review aim, ending with the objective or review question. You could incorporate the ideas listed here for other types of papers that require a background section; they are not specific to literature review introductions. And, if your literature review is only a short introduction, such as the background section for a research manuscript, then the following will be all you need from this chapter.

In the introduction or background section, you may use overview material that came up in your initial scoping searches, such as by citing existing relevant literature reviews. You may also have set aside some publications that came up in your literature review that you wanted to cite as background papers (see Chapter 4). Or you may have identified the most cited articles for the research area.

If you are writing a stand-alone piece with a background section and a results section, avoid using the background section to talk about publications that are included in your literature review. Your Includes will be documented in detail in the results section. It will be confusing for the reader if you mention some of the Includes in the background section when they are already the subject of your detailed literature review.

Note that you must be mindful of word limits, and you may have to select only a few aspects for the introduction and concentrate on these. Keep your audience in mind when you write the background section, as this will influence what kind of information you present, at what scientific level you do so, and how detailed you are.

Introductory Definitions

In the background section, define the topic you are reviewing, introduce the terminology you are working with, and state the context for your review. There might be more than one definition of the relevant psychological concepts. Also, different research fields may use unique terminology. You want to ensure that the reader understands where you are coming from.

Conceptual Introduction

The introduction is the place to explain to or remind the reader what concepts need to be differentiated to understand the research area and what phenomena have been addressed. You can describe what the research dilemmas are and what issues researchers have tackled as well as any practical or policy issues that make this area worth investigating. You might want to provide some historic background, outline how the research topic developed, and explain the current issues. You can introduce conflicting hypotheses that you came across or outline theories that have been suggested that can help tie the research together.

Introducing the State of the Research

It is also informative for your reader to understand the broad characteristics of the research field. This can be very basic information such as whether the research area is large or small. You can indicate this in the text or a visualization. One excellent way to document the literature is by creating a figure that plots the publication year of citations you have retrieved. This figure would document phases of interest in the research topic and the current research volume. This type of *metadata* (data about data) is readily available from some research databases. Or you can use your citation management program to export the publication year of all the citations that you found in your search and plot them in a graph. Figure 1 in the introduction chapter is an example of such a graph.

Introducing the Relevance of the Topic
and the Need for a Review

In the introduction, demonstrate why the topic is important—its significance may not be obvious to all readers. Here you could cite statistics
about the frequency of the problem you are addressing, describe the
burden of the clinical condition to individuals, describe the relevance of
the issue to society, or show how other areas are affected by the topic you
are reviewing. Ideally, give a rationale for the review and demonstrate why
your review is needed. This can be best done when you have checked other
reviews on the topic and are confident that you are reviewing something
novel or that existing reviews are outdated or otherwise inadequate to
answer your unique review question (see Chapter 1 for tips about exploring a potential topic).

Literature Review Objective and Review Questions

It is best to end the background section with a paragraph describing the
objective of the review. Here, you are summarizing why your review is
worth reading. The objective should state the review question you wanted
to answer. It should also incorporate information about the scope of the
review. Whereas the method section of the literature review documents
exactly what kind of information you were looking for, the objective should
paraphrase this information. The objective paragraph should broadly
summarize the review scope and be explicit about what the review will
and will not cover. It will help the reader a lot to have this summarized in
one paragraph before you launch into the methods and results.

METHOD SECTION OF YOUR LITERATURE REVIEW

For a stand-alone literature review project, it is best to add a separate
method section where you describe the review procedure, just as you
would do in any kind of research study write-up. This is your chance to
explain what you did and how you went about finding material for your
literature review. Depending on the overall literature review project

specification, this section might be placed separately in an appendix rather than the main text. For other literature review projects, a method section may simply be too much for the write-up; nonetheless, it can be very helpful to keep your documentation as a reminder of the methods and procedures and the many decisions you made during the review process.

Search and Source Documentation

A literature review should be able to state the sources clearly, particularly the databases that were searched and the date of the searches. A way to visualize the search as well as the review question is to show a Venn diagram that differentiates the elements that describe the review topic (see Chapter 3 for an example). In terms of documenting the search you should consider adding the search strings for at least one database to the appendix of the review write-up so that the reader knows how you went about searching for the topic.

Eligibility Criteria Documentation

The eligibility criteria should also be clearly stated, either summarized in the text or documented in detail in the appendix, using a framework such as PI/EMS (Population, Independent variable or Intervention/Exposure, Measure, and Study design). You can use a bulleted format with one bullet for each domain and, ideally, cover the inclusion and exclusion criteria for each domain.

Data Abstraction, Critical Appraisal, and Synthesis Methods

The description of the data abstraction process can be very brief. But any kind of data manipulation that you have undertaken should be described clearly. For example, you might have converted all results reported in individual studies to a common metric (e.g., counts converted to proportions or percentages).

The critical appraisal dimensions you have used should also be listed. But any scoring rules (e.g., how you decided whether a dimension had a high or low risk of bias) should probably go into the appendix. Although the detail is important, this kind of information is often too disruptive for the text flow. A bulleted format is also a good idea for this information.

Finally, you should explain your synthesis approach here, including the variables that you used to summarize the studies (e.g., you may have differentiated interventions V and W and the outcomes X, Y, and Z). This part describes your unique *review angle*, or how you have approached the literature.

RESULTS SECTION OF YOUR LITERATURE REVIEW

The results section is the key section of your literature review. It summarizes the search and inclusion screening results, uses the data extraction and the assessment of individual studies, and then presents the results of your synthesis. All parts of the review come together in the results section. In general, it is helpful to use the three-part structure described in the synthesis section (literature flow, included studies, results across studies).

Literature Flow Results

The first part of the results section should describe the literature flow and how many publications are included in the review. In some cases, you may need to put this information in an appendix or leave it out altogether, but generally, providing the reader with this kind of bigger picture will make your literature summary much more transparent. The clearest way to document the results of the inclusion screening decisions is a flow diagram (see Chapter 5 for a template). The literature flow diagram provides some information about the overall research field because it states the initial search yield, then shows how many publications you have looked at as full text, and finally, shows how many of those you ended up including in your review.

Individual Includes Overview

The most transparent way to document the publications that you are including in your literature review (i.e., part two of the synthesis) is to provide the reader with a brief table. This table is called an evidence table in literature reviews. As discussed in Chapter 8, an evidence table summarizes basic information about the Includes, that is, the material of your review. For you as the author of the review, putting the evidence table together will be helpful because it structures and organizes your material. For the reader, it is a way to get an instant overview, which will help the reader follow your conclusions about the literature. The table should be accompanied by a description of the study characteristics across studies. Depending on the type of the review and the length of the table, this table may go in the results section or the appendix or be left out altogether (even if you used it to structure your review).

The evidence table can include the critical appraisal results (if undertaken). Alternatively, the critical appraisal could be a separate table with a row for each study and a column for each critical appraisal dimension, and the table could state whether the appraisal criterion was met or not met. You can also use symbols or color-coding. A figure could plot the results across studies. Alternatively, you could summarize the critical appraisal results in the text (but you should have the information somewhere in tabular format in your own records).

Findings Across Includes—Synthesis

The third part of the results section should be dedicated to the synthesis of results across studies. This is the most important part of your literature review. Here, a summary of findings table can provide structure and organization and help the reader follow what you are showing. The summary of findings table superimposes the framework that you have used to synthesize the findings. For example, you might have ordered the empirical studies by outcome measure (see Chapter 8 for other suggestions for organizational schemes). Make sure to keep the table brief; it is a tool for an overview, not details, and some information may need to go into an appendix if necessary. Table 9.1 shows a completed summary of findings

Table 9.1

Example of a Completed Summary of Findings Table

Validity and application type Type of data	Number and type of studies (Number of participants) Reference	Findings	Body of evidence quality
	Review question: What is the validity of Rubin's Four Tendencies?		
Validation studies			
Any outcome data	1 book (conceptual work; Rubin, 2017), 1 survey (N = 1,564; data from Kirk, MacDonald, Lavender, Dean, & Rubin, 2017)	Descriptive model of four personality tendencies (Upholder, Questioner, Obliger, Rebel), not validated other than through face validity	Very low (study limitations: very little information is available on the identified study; not replicated in another study yet)
Application in research			
Any outcome data	1 case study (N = 1; Kirk, MacDonald, Lavender, Dean, & Rubin, 2017)	The case study describes a successful intervention to increase adherence to dietary advice; the intervention was based on applying the personality model	Very low (study limitations: case series; not replicated in another study yet)

Note. Searches based on PsycINFO, PsycARTICLES, PubMed, Google Scholar, and reference-mining in January 2019.

for a personality type model. The review author in our example first looked at validity studies, then applications in research. Very little literature was found; in fact, the review demonstrates how a topic from popular science might measure up to a literature reviewer's critical appraisal. With a larger research area, the review author could differentiate outcome measures (for what is there evidence, what exactly is being measured). The first column shows the review question, the type of research (validation, application), and the outcome. For each outcome, the table shows the number of studies, the number of participants, and the reference. One column summarizes the results across all identified studies for this type of research and data, and the last column evaluates the body of evidence and how confident the author can be in the documented results.

As discussed in detail in the previous chapter, here you do not want to summarize one study after the other but synthesize and show the reader what you have learned across studies. You may also communicate your confidence in the results (see the Quality of the Body of Evidence section in Chapter 8 for more details). Finally, make sure that you come back to the review question and answer it.

DISCUSSION SECTION OF YOUR LITERATURE REVIEW

In a stand-alone literature review, you are likely to include a discussion section. But as before, the format for your write-up depends on the specific instructions you have. Some journals, for example, prefer a combined results and discussion section for scientific articles. The following describes a possible structure for a separate discussion section. You may have to keep a word limit for your review in mind, and you may need to limit your discussion section to a few points from the following suggestions rather than cover everything.

A straightforward way to structure the discussion section is to start with a brief summary of the results, then give some indication of the quality of evidence. Next, discuss points in more detail that are worth highlighting to the reader, and put the results of your review in the context of other reviews where possible. Finally, acknowledge limitations, discuss the implications, make recommendations for future research, and end with a conclusion.

Summary of Findings

You can start your discussion section with a very brief overview of the answer to the review question. This will serve as a gentle reminder to the reader of what you wanted to find out and, very broadly, what the principal results are. In most cases, the summary of the results should not be longer than a couple of sentences; otherwise it will be repetitive (because there is a detailed results section) and distracting (the discussion should discuss, not just repeat).

Quality of Evidence

The discussion section is also a good place to come back to the quality of evidence assessment and your confidence in the findings. Your review will document results you found in the literature, but you do not need to take them all at face value. You can indicate where there are problems with the literature that make it hard to come up with a definitive answer. For example, the majority of studies may show one thing, but some studies may show the opposite. Or perhaps there are multiple studies, but they are all unique so each approach is essentially not replicated yet. You can combine this aspect with the next one or make them both separate points.

Interesting Discussion Points

The point-by-point discussion is the place to highlight some of the findings and to discuss them in more detail, interpret them, and potentially speculate about the reasons for certain results. You can either weave existing overview articles and systematic reviews into this or make a separate point showing how your review fits into the published reviews.

Putting the Results in Context

Try to get back to material that you used in your background section. Where does your review fit into the literature? Do you come to similar conclusions compared with an existing review? Or point out what is special about your review.

Limitations

Your review should have a limitations section. This section should state limitations of the evidence base as well as limitations of your review. Limitations of the evidence base have to do with the literature that you found or did not find (i.e., important research that is lacking from the literature according to your review). But you should also point out some limitations of your review. In a stand-alone literature review, readers will expect you to disclose the limitations of your work. For example, other areas could contribute to the review question but were outside the scope of your review. You will likely have had to restrict your search to a couple of central databases, so some material may have been missed. You have narratively summarized the results of the Includes, but only a meta-analysis could provide a pooled estimate of the effect across studies. And so on. There is no need to disparage your review and your work, but try to think about a couple of key limitations to communicate to the reader (the reader might not know what the issues could be).

Implications for Practice

It will be helpful for the reader to know what you think are the implications that follow from the results of your literature review. Here you can think about implications for practice and policy. But in this section either make sure that you are not going beyond your literature review results (e.g., don't make statements about areas that you haven't reviewed) or clarify that you are merely speculating.

Future Research

Another key area in a literature review is making recommendations about future research. Informing future research may even be one of the main goals of a literature review. There may have not been sufficient studies to answer the review questions, and it will be helpful to point out exactly which and what kind of studies are missing to adequately address the review questions. Consider plotting the presence and absence of information in a table grid; that way the gaps in the currently literature will be most obvious.

In Figure 9.2 you see an example of how you could plot the presence and the absence of research. The grid differentiates three study populations and shows how many studies there are (represented by the blobs) for one outcome. This kind of visualization makes it very clear where research is missing.

The future research section will be most informative when you are specific; don't just end by saying "more research is needed." Usually, it is best to address future research needs in a framework; it can be the same framework that you have used for your eligibility criteria. Using a framework structures this kind of *gap analysis* and ensures that you are specific and concrete in what is needed.

Population	Measure 1 (e.g., morning alertness)
1 (e.g., children)	
2 (e.g., teenagers)	◕◕
3 (e.g., adults)	◕◕◕◕◕◕

Figure 9.2

Evidence gap map. ◕ denotes research study.

Conclusion

It is a good idea to end the discussion with a conclusion section (rather than end with a limitation or implication section). In this short take-home message for the reader, you can note what you found out with your literature review. For example, it can be a combination of the summary of findings, implications, and future research needs. You can make this longer than a sentence, but you do want to keep this section brief.

BIBLIOGRAPHY SECTION OF YOUR LITERATURE REVIEW

The bibliography or reference section should include all the publications you are citing in the text. It needs to be complete, and that is why it is best to work with a citation management program (cite as you write; see Chapter 5). On the other hand, this section can include only the publications that you have cited in the text. Do not add papers that you have identified but then did not use for your literature review. If the publication is important, think of a way to add it to your review so that you can cite it in the text.

The bibliography section needs to be formatted according to the style specified in the assignment. If no style is specified, use APA Style. Note that the formatting is much easier when you work with a citation management program. Rather than editing each citation, you just tell the program which reference style you want to use, and it will format them all for you.

APPENDIX SECTION OF YOUR LITERATURE REVIEW

An appendix can be a great way to provide more details on the methodology without interrupting the text flow of the review. For example, the full search strategy would go in the appendix, as shown in Figure 9.3.

Appendix: Search strategy
Date: 10/28/2018

Database: PubMed
((flow experienc*) OR "optimal experience" OR (concentration great absorption
experienc*) OR Csikszentmihalyi) AND child*
Results: 22

Database: PsycINFO
((flow experienc*) OR "optimal experience" OR (concentration AND absorption AND
experienc*) OR Csikszentmihalyi) AND child*
Option: Phrase Searching (Boolean)
Results: 145

Figure 9.3

Example appendix page for search strategy.

The literature flow diagram could go in the text or in the appendix. Where appropriate, even the full list of excluded publications could be presented here so that an interested reader could see what publications you ultimately considered to be outside of the review scope. The evidence table is also often best placed in the appendix, given that tables longer than two pages may interrupt the text flow too much. Although an overview figure of the critical appraisal result is great for the text, the detailed methods and results are also often best placed in the appendix. If you have formally assessed the body of evidence, you may want to use an appendix to outline your criteria and any information that did not fit in the main text or summary of findings table.

ADDITIONAL RESOURCES AND INSTRUCTIONS

The above provides you with an outline for how you can document your literature review, but keep in mind that there may be other resources you could use. Various organizations publish guidance for different types of stand-alone literature reviews (see the Helpful Resources box).

For systematic reviews, the methods and results need to be documented in detail because the ultimate goal is for the reader to follow the conclusions of the review author. The PRISMA group provides a checklist that helps authors to remember all the items that are relevant for reporting a systematic review. The reporting structure can be useful for all reviews.

Helpful Resources

PRISMA (Preferred Reporting Items for Systematic Reviews and Meta-Analyses) provides a reporting checklist and a flow diagram that are used by many systematic reviews and endorsed by many journals (http://prisma-statement.org; see the Key Documents section).

There are also APA Style Journal Article Reporting Standards (JARS) for different study designs to support journal publications (see http://www.apastyle.org/jars), including guidance for meta-analyses (see https://www.apastyle.org/manual/related/JARS-MARS.pdf).

Finally, you may decide to report the results of your review in more than one outlet, such as an internal research report and a journal manuscript. Note that the APA and many journals have specific reporting guidelines that you need to follow. For example, there is an APA reporting guideline for meta-analyses, and JARS-Qual (see https://www.apastyle.org/jars/qualitative) includes a section on qualitative meta-analysis reporting.

This concludes your literature review. Hurray!

CHAPTER 9 ACTION STEPS

☐ Determine the best format for the methods and detail documentation of your review (e.g., in the text, in the appendix, in a separate document).

☐ Structure your review by using ideas presented in this chapter.

☐ Consider using tables and figures to document your literature review.

Further Reading

This section contains recommendations for further reading on systematic reviews, meta-analyses, reviews of reviews (umbrella reviews), and scoping reviews.

BOOKS

Biondi-Zoccai, G. (Ed.). (2016). *Umbrella reviews*. Cham, Switzerland: Springer.

Cooper H., Hedges L. V., & Valentine, J. C. (Eds.). (2009). *The handbook of research synthesis and meta-analysis* (2nd ed.). New York, NY: Russell Sage Foundation.

Petticrew, M., & Roberts, H. (2006). *Systematic reviews in the social sciences: A practical guide*. Malden, MA: Blackwell.

JOURNAL ARTICLES AND ONLINE REPORTS

Arksey, H., & O'Malley, L. (2003). Scoping studies: Towards a methodological framework. *International Journal of Social Research Methodology, 8*(1), 19–32. http://dx.doi.org/10.1080/1364557032000119616

Centre for Reviews and Dissemination. (2009). *Systematic reviews: CRD's guidance for undertaking reviews in health care*. York, England: University of York. Retrieved from http://www.york.ac.uk/inst/crd/SysRev/!SSL!/WebHelp/SysRev3.htm

Glass, G. V. (2014). Meta-analysis at middle age: A personal history. *Research Synthesis Methods, 6*, 221–231. http://dx.doi.org/10.1002/jrsm.1133

LIVING DOCUMENTS

Agency for Healthcare Research and Quality. (2014). *Methods guide for effectiveness and comparative effectiveness reviews* (Publication No. 10(14)-EHC063-EF). Retrieved from https://effectivehealthcare.ahrq.gov/topics/cer-methods-guide/overview

Higgins, J. P. T., & Green, S. (Eds.). (2011). *Cochrane handbook for systematic reviews of interventions* (Version 5.1.0, updated March 2011). The Cochrane Collaboration. Retrieved from http://handbook-5-1.cochrane.org

SUGGESTIONS FROM INDIVIDUAL CHAPTERS

Chapter 4

Shadish, W. R., Cook, T. D., & Campbell, D. T. (2001). *Experimental and quasi-experimental designs for generalized causal inference* (2nd ed.). Boston, MA: Houghton Mifflin Company.

Urban, J. B., & Van Eeden-Moorefield, B. M. (2018). *Designing and proposing your research project.* Washington, DC: American Psychological Association.

Chapter 6

Field, A., Miles, J., & Field, Z. (2012). *Discovering statistics using R.* Chicago, IL: Sage.

Chapter 8

Cooper, H. (2017). Research synthesis and meta-analysis: A step-by-step approach (5th ed.). Thousand Oaks, CA: Sage.

Miles, J. N. V., & Banyard, P. (2007). Understanding and using statistics in psychology: A practical introduction. London, England: Sage.

Chapter 9

American Psychological Association. (2020). *Publication manual of the American Psychological Association* (7th ed.). https://doi.org/10.1037/0000165-000

Index

About the Author

Susanne Hempel, PhD, is a psychologist directing the Southern California Evidence-Based Practice Center, a center that produces literature reviews for federal funding agencies. She is a senior behavioral scientist at RAND, a professor of social science at the Pardee RAND Graduate School, a professor of research preventive medicine at the University of Southern California (USC), and a faculty member at the Gehr Center for Health Systems Science at USC. She lives in Los Angeles with her husband, teenaged twins, and many animals.

About the Series Editor

Arthur M. Nezu, PhD, DHL, ABPP, is Distinguished University Professor of Psychology, professor of medicine, and professor of public health at Drexel University. He is currently editor-in-chief of *Clinical Psychology: Science and Practice*, as well as former editor of the *Journal of Consulting and Clinical Psychology* and *The Behavior Therapist*. He also served as an associate editor for *American Psychologist* and the *Archives of Scientific Psychology*. Additional editorial positions include chair of the American Psychological Association's (APA's) Council of Editors, member of the advisory committee for APA's *Publication Manual,* and member of the task force to revise APA's journal article reporting standards for quantitative research. His research and program development have been supported by the National Cancer Institute, the National Institute of Mental Health, the Department of Veterans Affairs, the Department of Defense, the U.S. Air Force, and the Pew Charitable Trusts. Dr. Nezu has also served on numerous research review panels for the National Institutes of Health and is a member of APA's Board of Scientific Affairs. He was former president of the Association for Behavioral and Cognitive Therapies and the American Board of Behavioral and Cognitive Psychology as well as the recipient of numerous awards for his research and professional contributions.